In the time I've known Jerry, he reminds me more and more of a bulldog. Once he gets a project between his teeth he just doesn't let up—which is an admirable quality for a celebrity publicist. Given a task, he lets nothing stand in the way of his accomplishing it. Hey, he even got me to write this paragraph! Good work, Jerry. Keep it up.

— **Stan Lee**

Albert Einstein once said, "Try not to become a man of success, but rather try to become a man of value". Someone who has achieved that is Jerry Olivarez. Armed only with a firmly held belief that he could accomplish anything he set his mind to, I witnessed Jerry's inspiring rise to prominence, working as a small town florist and later rising to become one of the most successful and admired people in the flashy world of high profile public relations. Through it all, Jerry remains an incredibly gracious, loyal and loving person who gives much of himself to those around him. Despite the celebrity circles he often finds himself moving in – Jerry remains refreshingly humble and centered. He is a man of true values and character with the gift of positive energy and natural charisma which people naturally gravitate towards.

Jerry's rags to riches story and his path to greatness is a moving tale that will inspire anyone to achieve greatness in their own life.

—**Michael Holmstrom**
President – Signature Parking Inc.

Jerry Olivarez is one of the most focused professionals I know. He looks at the longterm, not letting temporary setbacks stop him. I don't recall a single instance in which he didn't follow through on something he said he would do. That is a rare thing in this business.

— **Alan Duke,**
CNN Digital Entertainment Editor

My Life on the Red Carpet:
He Grew Into the Suit

Jerry Olivarez

Circumference Press

Copyright © 2015 by Jerry Olivarez
Published by Circumference Press

All rights reserved. This book may not be used or reproduced in any manner, in whole or in part, stored in a retrieval system or transmitted in any form (by electronic, mechanical, photocopied, recorded or other means) without written permission from the author, except as permitted by United States copyright law.

No liability is assumed with respect to the use of information contained herein. While every precaution has been taken in the preparation of this book, the author assumes no responsibility for errors or omissions. Neither is any liability assumed for damages resulting from the use of information contained herein.

Cover art by Scott Simson

Cover Photo by Lily Dong
www.LilyDongPhotography.com

Editing and layout by Jonathan Peters, PhD

ISBN: 978-0-9789229-4-8

Printed in the United States of America

www.JerryOlivarez.com

Acknowledgements

I wish to acknowledge the following list of people for the importance they've played in my life and their contribution to my life story and this book. It's a long list, but not long enough. I fear I've missed some names:

Stan Lee, Howard Weitzman, Bill Hertz, Alan Duke, Rocco Bialie, George Maloof, Neda Barry, Perry Sanders, Jack Dudum, Tony Dudum, J.J. Dudum, Trevor Groth, Adam Baca, Dennis Hopper, Dr. Campos, Dr. Charles Kasper, Dr. Hersh, Dr. Timothy Carlton, Walter Eichinger, La Toya Jackson, Danny Greenspun, Robin Greenspun, Oprah Winfrey, Ken Miller, Howard Tarmino, b.b. Simon, Joey Cappuccino, Claire Kirchen, Sue Rieck, Bobby Slayton, Brian Diperstein, Lolek, Michael Holmstrom, Terry Salmon, John McAdams, Timothy Howard, Kirk Schenck, Katherine Jackson, Joe Jackson, Mike Smith, Wendy Smith, Jerome Picot, Christina Gates, Chris Tishue, Stu Alson, Brad Corcron, Mark Peterson, Brian Kaskie, Melanie Purnell, Lily Dong, Travis Lodes, William Agular, Mark Mochey, Matt Bolinger, Mr. Escobar, Kyle Williams, Brad Coffman, Jason Griego, Michael Griego, Vincent Castrillo, Mark Howard, Justin Alterman, Brian Alterman, Billy Tonkovich, Brian Peterson, Steve Tyler, Raymone Bain, Steve Haworth, Ken Haworth, Mike Moneice, Sukhdip Singh, Lowell Henry.

And a special thanks to Jonathan Peters, PhD, without whom this book would not have been possible.

CONTENTS

Foreword by Robin Leach ... 1
Chapter 1: Outside, Looking In ... 5
Chapter 2: When I Grow Up, I Want to be a... ... 9
Chapter 3: Becoming a Florist ... 15
Chapter 4: Meeting Al Pacino ... 19
Chapter 5: Pro Forma ... 23
Chapter 6: Opening My Own Shop ... 29
Chapter 7: The Rich Get Richer ... 33
Chapter 8: Meeting Oprah Winfrey ... 37
Chapter 9: Go to the Top ... 47
Chapter 10: Meeting Carol Burnett ... 51
Chapter 11: David and Goliath ... 53
Chapter 12: The Yellow Pages ... 59
Chapter 13: Getting the Story Corrected ... 63
Chapter 14: Meeting Johnny Brenden ... 65
Chapter 15: Dress for Success ... 73
Chapter 16: Next Steps ... 77
Chapter 17: New York City ... 81
Chapter 18: A Changing Industry ... 85
Chapter 19: Changing Directions ... 89
Chapter 20: A Personal Publicist ... 93

CONTENTS

Chapter 21: Meeting Bill Hertz   97
Chapter 22: Meeting Robin Leach   103
Chapter 23: Putting on a Premiere   107
Chapter 24: The Brenden Celebrity Suite   113
Chapter 25: Brenden Celebrity Star   119
Chapter 26: Visiting the Mansion   127
Chapter 27: The infamous O.J. Simpson   131
Chapter 28: Honored by the First Lady of California: Maria Shriver   137
Chapter 29: What Love Is: The Movie   141
Chapter 30: Devastating News   145
Chapter 31: Success is About Showing Up   149
Chapter 32: "Rocky Balboa": the compromise   153
Chapter 33: Getting an Aisle Seat   157
Chapter 34: Meeting the king of pop   159
Chapter 35: Michael's Celebrity Star   165
Chapter 36: Invitation to Sacramento State   169
Chapter 37: This is It   175
Chapter 38: Two for the money   183
Chapter 39: A Cautionary Tale   189

CONTENTS

Chapter 40: Stan Lee's Greatest Creation — 191

Chapter 41: Michael Jackson Commemorative Belt — 197

Chapter 42: Being Let Go — 207

Chapter 43: George Clooney & Stan Lee — 213

Chapter 44: SendHerFlowers.com — 217

Chapter 45: Hollywood Walk of Fame — 223

Chapter 46: Going Back to Indiana: Can You Feel It? Michael Jackson's Celebration — 231

Chapter 47: First Annual Giants' Stan Lee Day at AT&T Park — 241

Chapter 48: Looking Back Looking Forward — 249

Dedication

This book is dedicated to the biggest influence and inspiration in my life, and two people who made me the man I am today: **my mother and father.**

Mom always made sure we had what we needed. Sometimes she had to cook five different breakfasts. She made sure we were in church, did our homework, and were in bed on time. She taught me unconditional love. I miss her.

Mom once said her family was her Rolls Royce, her mansion, and her diamonds. In loving memory of the most wonderful person I have ever known, my beloved mother.

Dad worked hard to provide for his family. Few men have the opportunity to work with their father as easily as I worked with mine. We were often admired for our mutual respect. He taught me so much about how to differentiate ourselves from the competition.

Dad, you taught me a lot, and all I had to do was watch you live your life.

A Special Thank-you to:

Johnny Brenden: Thank you for coming into my life, believing in me, and for your friendship. I will forever be indebted.

Walter Eichinger, Exec. VP of Operations for Brenden Theatre Corp: I have known you for over 25 years, and I have the utmost respect for you. You have the finest employees in the movie theater industry, which is a true testament to the respect your employees have for you. I am proud to call you my friend, and I thank you for your continued support.

Robin Leach: Thank you so much for writing my foreword and for your friendship. I will always value it.

Ted Mann: Johnny Brendens grandfather, pioneer in the movie theatre industry. Thank you for our private conversations and your encouragement and support.

Jack Gilardi: Thank you for your friendship.

Elaine Kendall: Thank you for your love, friendship, and support.

JC Lee: Thank you for your friendship, loyalty, and for always having my back. I love you.

Joe Girouard: Thank you so much for your excellent support, your loyalty, and for your encouragement to write this book.

Greg Warner: Thank you for your mentoring.

Yvonne Warner: Thank you for your friendship, love, and believing in me, and for raising two of the most amazing boys.

Jack Warner: My God son, I am so proud of the young man you turned out to be. And thank you for your love.

Scott Warner: My God son, I am so proud of you. Thank you for your love.

Kellen Smith: My God son, I am so proud of you and all of your accomplishments. Thank you for being in my life and for your love.

Ryan Smith: Thank you for coming into my life, for your love, and for inviting me to speak to your class for Professor Howard at Sacramento State University. You where my inspiration to write this book and for giving me the opportunity to see the impact that my mentoring had on you. Thank You for your continued support and love.

Louie Bright: My intern, my family, and one that I mentor. I am so proud of you, thank you for your love and support.

Simon Tavassoli of b.b. Simon: My friend and business partner, one of the most passionate and talented people I have ever met. Thank you for believing in me, trusting my judgement, and for supporting me. We did it!

Peter Voutsas of Peter Marco Jeweler (252 N. Rodeo Dr. Beverly Hills, CA 90210, 310-278-5353): My friend for loving my ties, buying my ties, and selling them in your beautiful store. You have no idea what you did for me by believing in my line of ties. You where the first retail store to carry my ties. Wow, my first store is on Rodeo Drive. Thank You.

Rocco Biale, the owner of Rocco's Restaurant. Once awarded Best Business Man in Walnut Creek. I have known Rocco for over 25 years, I am Proud and Lucky to call him my friend and confidant. Thank you for all you do. With much respect.

Dr. Timothy Howard, Professor, Sacramento State University. I once received an invitation to speak to a few college students; little did I know it would change my life. I thank you for your gracious invitation to speak to your PRSSA students of Sacramento State University. I thank you even more for asking me to return for a second time. That meant so much to me. You and your students were the catalyst and inspiration in writing this book. Thank you for providing the mechanism that has fueled one of the most rewarding experiences of my life. I will forever cherish this experience on both a professional and personal level. I stand humbled by your success and the numerous achievements your dedication to the industry has provided the future minds of our great profession. Long live accuracy, brevity and clarity.

And With Much Love and Respect to...

My big sister Chris, mother of three (Andre, Erica, and Freddy), who is like a mother to all of us. I love Chris with all my heart.

My big brother Oscar, father to Alissa Marie, I idolized him as my big brother. Growing up, I wanted to be with him, hang out with him, and follow him around. His friends referred to me as his shadow. He passed away too young at 48. I miss him everyday.

My older sister Terry, mother to three boys (Richie, Ray, and Ryan). She keeps everyone on their toes. Yes, she's a bit of a rebel, but she would do anything for us. I love her.

My younger sister Audrey, mother to Audrey, Krystal, and Jorge. I remember when she was born. I thought it was so cool to have a baby sister. She was a beautiful baby and is an even more lovely adult. I love her.

My nephew Jorge. I could live to be 150 years old and I could never thank him enough for taking care of my father. Without this young man, I could not do what I do. I love him more than words could ever express.

My niece Audrey. I am so proud of this little girl. She was able to put herself through an elite epicurean school, le Cordon Bleu of San Francisco. She has been working three jobs and taking public transportation. She is a huge inspiration to me.

My niece Krystal. She put herself through beauty school and also helped with my mom and dad. I love you.

My mom, dad, and I, in a small way, helped raise these kids. I love them as if they were my children, and there is nothing I would not do for them.

Foreword

My Life on the Red Carpet is a fascinating, entertaining, and informative look at the celebrity world, both on and off the famed red carpets of movie premieres, star ceremonies, and platinum parties.

Celebrity publicist Jerry Olivarez has the inside stories of his time, involving a host of celebrities, including Michael Jackson and the Jackson family, George Clooney, Stan Lee, Sylvester Stallone, and Maria Shriver, just to name a few. Jerry is a confidante of America's top silver-screen personalities and, until now, he's kept all those secrets under wraps.

Jerry's book is filled with celebrity encounters, humorous anecdotes, sincere words of wisdom, and momentous experiences, including stories of heart-warming moments with Oprah Winfrey at the Jackson family's home, with Stan Lee at the ballpark, and so much more. Jerry knows them all, from Playboy mogul Hugh Hefner to music superstar Kid Rock, to actor Cuba Gooding Jr.

Jerry not only reveals how he's maneuvered the backstage green rooms, but also his battles with TV reporters and tabloid journalists, in order to protect his favorite stars. Jerry has always gone above and beyond the call of duty; his exciting stories make that clear.

Better yet, Jerry shares the details of his journey from his humble beginnings as a florist to his more recent successes as a publicist, event producer, and entrepreneur. Along the way, he provides readers with professional insight, including advice on how to create a business plan, how to value customers and clients, and how to network and build relationships.

If you have ever wanted to peak inside the world of celebrities, or have even wondered what it's like to work on the "inside" with the stars themselves, then *My Life on the Red Carpet* is your must-read book. Enjoy the ride with my good friend, Jerry.

Champagne wishes to the red carpet commander and commando!

—Robin Leach
Lifestyles of the Rich and Famous

My Life on the Red Carpet

CHAPTER 1

OUTSIDE, LOOKING IN

When I was young, every Sunday at 4:00 PM, was my time to lie on the living room floor and watch my favorite program.

The show was *Lifestyles of the Rich and Famous*, hosted by Robin Leach. Every week I'd marvel with amazement at where Robin Leach would take us. He'd show us celebrities' amazing homes and their exotic cars.

I would imagine what it would be like to live in that environment. But that was a long way away from my neighborhood in Northern California.

Right out of high school, my best friend, Terry Salmon, asked me if I'd like to take a trip to L.A. We did all the usual tourist things like going to Disneyland and Knots Berry Farm, and looking at all the stars along the Hollywood Walk of Fame.

We also visited the world-famous Mann's Chinese Theatre where we stood in front of the famous lion statues and took pictures next to the different handprints and footprints. We marveled at all of the movie stars who had walked the red carpet before entering the theater.

Afterwards, Terry and I stood on Rodeo Drive watching all these expensive cars drive by. I thought to myself, who are those people in the Rolls Royces, Ferraris, and Porches? What was their story? Would I ever meet them?

As the decades passed, I forgot about that childhood trip and my question about whether I'd ever meet celebrities and the rich and famous.

Then one day, the memory came firing back.

I was at a stop light on Rodeo Drive with Johnny Brenden. We were in his canary-yellow Lamborghini Murciélago. I looked out my window and saw two kids standing on the corner. They were looking at the blackened window, trying to see who was inside.

In that moment, I had come full circle. I saw myself as one of those kids. I literally saw the car through their eyes. I remembered what it was like: the wonder, the desire.

And here I was, one of those people in an exotic car, sitting next to one of those people I had wondered if I'd ever meet. In fact, I was in the car of Ted Mann's grandson. It was Ted Mann whose theater I had stood outside of as a teenager checking out the handprints of famous people.

It was a surreal moment.

As the memories jumped forward, I remembered how Terry and I had stood in the lobby of the Beverly Hills Hotel. I imagined what it would be like to stay there overnight. And just the night before, I had spent yet another evening in a luxurious suite at the very same hotel.

Back then, I was an outsider to the glamour of Hollywood. Now I was attending premieres, walking the red carpets ,and shaking hands with celebrities.

In fact, at the very moment I was in the Lamborghini on my way to meet the president of Fox Studios.

The journey that brought me from outside the Lamborghini to inside is an exciting one, and one I am grateful to be able to share.

But this is not a rags to riches story. I enjoy my lifestyle now because of the groundwork I laid as a young man. While good fortune brought me to where I am today, it wasn't just luck. Yes, many generous people have helped me along the way, preparing me for the amazing experiences I've had.

I am able to sit in a Lamborghini on Rodeo Drive because many years ago, I learned lessons, applied principles, and worked hard to manifest my goals and dreams.

As you read these pages, please don't put me on a pedestal. While I have had an amazing life, lived spectacular experiences, and have no regrets, you too can accomplish what I've accomplished, and so much more.

After all, I started humbly with a goal to have a successful flower shop. Over time, of course, my vision expanded greatly. However, what I'd like to emphasize are the things I've learned along the way that established the person I am today.

I share my insights and experiences in the hopes that from my life you will gain inspiration and have the tools you need to achieve the most outstanding dreams you can envision.

Chapter 2

When I Grow Up, I Want to Be A...

Back when I was a child, we knew we were struggling, but we didn't have much to compare ourselves to. We saw rich people on television, but we weren't aware of the vast difference between us and them.

When my dad had an accident in 1968, we lived in Danville, California. After several operations and after being pronounced dead a few times, my father not only survived, but was also able to provide for his family for years to come.

I'm sure I will never fully understand the hardship my parents experienced following the accident, but we were never hungry. We were clean, and we were dressed in good clothes. We did however, survive on the food church members would bring to our house. And Christmas was a magical time because of the toys others brought us.

Even in this environment, my mom always said, "Jerry, you can do whatever you want in life. All you have to do is visualize it. You have to be grateful, and thank God as if you have already received it. Feel the emotion of having what it is you want or being the person you want to be."

Most boys aspire to do spectacular things when they grow up, like become astronauts, policemen, firemen, and so on. When I was ten, I told a buddy that when I grew up, I was going to become a florist like my father.

I have this photo framed in my office with the caption: "Jerry Olivarez, Executive Director of Public Relations, Brenden Theatre Corporation." It puts things into perspective. The picture was taken in 1963. I was two years old with my dad and my dog Spot. I've come a long way.

When I grow up, I want to be...

Why? Because back then, boys were expected to follow in their fathers' footsteps, and my father was a renowned florist. He was awarded for being one of the top florists in the country at the Empress of China in San Francisco. He received a standing ovation for every one of his presentations at the flower show.

As I write this, I am overwhelmed with emotion. My father is now 78 years old and not in the best of health. This man provided for his family and has given the shirt off his back for not only his friends, but strangers as well. Following his accident, he didn't feel sorry for himself; instead, he applied himself, worked hard, and continued to seize opportunities.

As a child, I enjoyed working with my father and watching him interact with his clients.

I particularly remember one of my father's clients who was an heiress to the Dodge corporation. He was her personal florist.

She was generous, and sent us gifts for our birthdays and different anniversaries. Throughout the year, my dad would bring home huge boxes of chocolates that she had given us. At Thanksgiving, she'd send us a turkey. She even gave us a color television one Christmas. But the best gift she ever gave my family was in 1971. I remember the excitement in my home when my dad announced that Mrs. Ranger had given us tickets to see Elvis Presley.

She was the first of them I knew well. Her generosity taught me that wealth is about more than accumulating; it is also about giving and sharing. I understood at that young age the joy she got from giving those gifts.

As I enjoy success, I remember her. She was a model of the joy that true wealth brings. While the finer things in life are important and exciting, nothing warms the heart more than sharing with others, especially with those who appreciate the gift.

I rushed home from first grade at Green Valley Elementary in Danville, CA to set up my snack stand. That's a red cash register in front of me. I sold soft drinks, candy bars, and frozen Kool-Aid my mom made for me in little paper Dixie cups, for 25 cents. I would have a line from my front porch to the sidewalk everyday. I remember one day I made $9.00. We went to the store so I could buy more inventory.

When I grow up, I want to be...

My first Holy Communion at St. Isidore Church in Danville, CA. Of course, I was at the front of the line; I was already a leader. I don't think it was because I was the shortest boy. Notice, I was a sharp dresser even back then.

CHAPTER 3

BECOMING A FLORIST

My eyes were opened to the lives of the wealthy when I was riding in the car with my dad.

My dad had a meeting with Ray outside of a coffee shop in Danville. As I sat in the car, I overheard their conversation. They were discussing something that Yvonne wanted.

As I listened, I learned that Ray was Yvonne's publicist. While I didn't understand everything they discussed, I remember thinking that I'd like to do what THAT GUY does. The life of the publicist seemed exciting.

That dream wouldn't come true for many years, but the seed had been planted. Over the years, I nourished it, tilling the soil, preparing the environment, so that it would bloom one day.

In the meantime, I learned the florist trade by constantly watching my father work. When I was 15, I told my

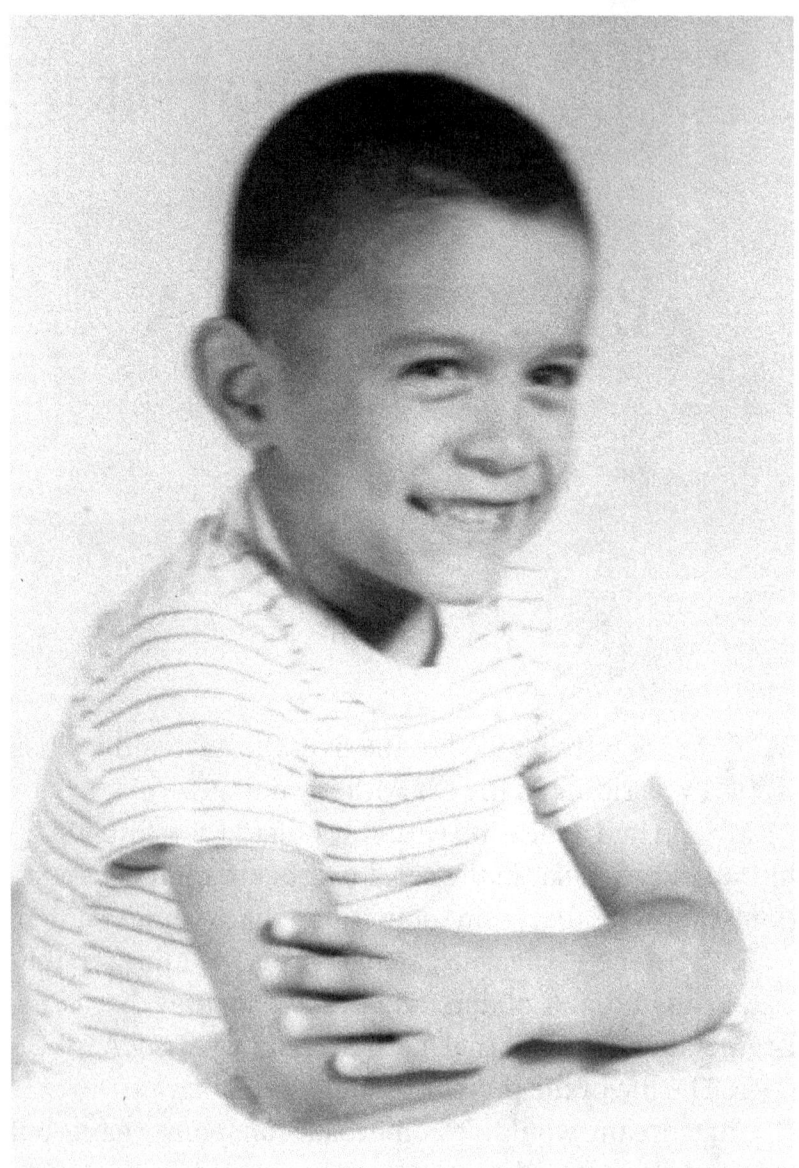

At age five, my mom took me to a Walgreen's type store that had a place where you could get your portrait taken. I remember the photographer asking me to smile. After, we went to the counter and Mom got me a milkshake. That was a good day.

dad that I wanted to work at a flower shop. He asked me, "What shop would you like to work at?"

I replied, "Lila's Florist," an extremely nice flower shop.

My father called the owner of the shop, Don Galloway. Because of my father's outstanding reputation and credibility, Don told my dad to have me come in.

When I got there, I was met by the general manager. The first words out of his mouth were, "Hi Jerry. Of course, you're already hired, but please fill out this application."

After that, I was on my way. I started out as a delivery boy, worked up to a designer, and then I became a manager of the store.

Over the years, I moved around a bit, landing jobs at different flower shops until finally arriving at Jory's Flowers in Walnut Creek, CA. I walked into the shop and introduced myself to the owner, Duane Hotton.

He said, "Your father is Oscar? I know him. That man is worth his weight in gold."

Wow. How nice to hear such praise about your father.

I was hired and worked for several years with Duane before opening my own flower shop. To this day, I maintain a friendly relationship with Duane. He works part-time for his son during the holidays, and he still likes to hear my red carpet stories when I visit.

As you read my stories, there are common threads: maintain integrity, be consistent, follow through, and have a clean reputation. As you can see, one's reputation precedes them. At the end of the day, that's all you have. Maintain it. Cherish it.

Over the years, I executed everything I set out to do. I never demanded that I be more than I was. At the same time, I strove for something more. I knew I was destined for something much greater, but in the meantime, I was more than happy to learn the lessons I was given.

Eventually, I sold my flower shop and joined another company.

From there, my career took an interesting turn thanks to Johnny Brenden. It's not everyone who can go from a florist to a Hollywood insider, but there is nothing unique about me. I work hard, and live by certain ideals, and life has brought me some exciting opportunities.

The reason I was ready for the opportunities that Johnny Brenden gave me is that I had worked hard when I was a young man. I had learned lessons along the way, and I had consciously prepared myself so that when opportunity came to me, I was ready to accept it.

And you have the same capacities. Given a few opportunities, while working hard, you can achieve more than I have.

Believe me, your Johnny Brenden is out there. While you wait for that blessing, prepare yourself now. You may get discouraged about where you are, but know that amazing opportunities are coming.

CHAPTER 4

MEETING AL PACINO

In my life, I've met some amazing people. One of my most exciting meetings was Al Pacino, because he is one of my favorite actors.

I was at the Four Seasons in Beverly Hills, sitting with a couple of girls. Suddenly I saw movement out of the corner of my eye. When I looked that way, I knew I needed to act.

I set down my drink and excused myself from the table.

"Mr. Pacino, my name is Jerry Olivarez. I appreciate all the work you've done."

Al Pacino shook my hand, and thanked me for my kind words.

I continued, "I just framed a picture of *Godfather 3*. I spent $750 on the framing of it."

He nodded.

I wanted to continue, to tell him how much I admired his work, but I forgot every movie he's ever done, like *Scent of a Woman*, one of my favorite movies. While I tried to recall even one of his movies, he shook my hand and said, "Thank you very much."

As he turned to walk away, I blurted, "Mr. Pacino, you just made my day."

He stopped, turned, land ooked at me. In that classic Pacino style, he pointed at me, and said, "And you just made my day." Then he pointed back at himself.

The reality is that I would have liked to have congratulated him on his Academy Award and let him know how much I like *Scent of a Woman*. I wish I could have told him how much he meant to me as an actor. But my mind was blank.

I've learned that when I meet celebrities, my mind often goes blank. I want to tell them their impact on my life and share with them the importance they have for their audiences, and yet, my mind goes blank in front of them. It doesn't matter how many important people I've met in my lifetime, my brain still blanks when I'm in the presence of greatness.

For instance, I was at a party in Beverly Hills, and Jim Belushi was there. I love his show, *Defenders*.

My friend, Alan Duke, from *CNN* was also at this party. He walked over to Jim, and said, "Do you know Jerry? He's the guy you need to know in Hollywood."

Jim turned to me, impressed by the introduction Alan had given me, and my mind went blank. I forgot the name of his show, who was in it, even when it came out.

I was disappointed because I wasn't able to tell him how much I appreciated his work.

Celebrity is an interesting phenomenon. I'm not sure why my mind goes blank when I'm in the presence of someone whom I admire, but it does show that person's impact on my life.

My Life on the Red Carpet

CHAPTER 5

PRO FORMA

In the early 1980s, when I was still at Jory's Flowers in Walnut Creek, Yvonne Warner came into the shop to discuss flowers for her wedding. I began showing her different arrangements, offering suggestions and ideas.

After 30 minutes she thanked me and said that she'd be shopping around a bit.

Of course, I knew she was going to check out other shops, but I also knew that no one would be able to compare to the arrangements I had shown her.

Less than an hour later, she was back in the shop. "I don't know why I'm shopping around. You know exactly what I want."

That day, we began our friendship. The wedding went flawlessly, and she loved the flowers. Even after the event, she still came by to order arrangements for different occasions.

One day when Yvonne was in the shop, she touched my arm and whispered, "If you ever want to open up a flower shop of your own, you let me know. I will put you in business."

It was a casual comment, but it stuck with me. What I learned later in life is that people will often come to you with offers of support before you are ready for them. It's like the universe is preparing you for the idea that you're ready to take the next step.

When good people see your dedication to your work and recognize your potential, they will reach out. They want to help you be successful. Yvonne understood my potential, and she encouraged me to take the next step even though it was a major one.

We stayed in touch, and time passed. The day came when I let her know that I was ready to open my own shop. She smiled and invited me to dinner at her home.

I was nervous going to their home. Interacting with Yvonne in the shop was one thing, going to her house was quite another. I was very aware that I was crossing a divide from provider of flowers to something more.

I was sweating when I rang the bell. Her husband opened the door. He was tall, and had graying hair, yet was young and athletic looking. He was well dressed, and had the demeanor of a man who had just stepped off his sailboat.

"Jerry," he said, extending his hand.

I had never met him before, but I already felt like a confidant. I accepted his hand. "Nice to meet you, Greg."

He smiled, "Yvonne tells me you want to be an entrepreneur."

I nodded, not really sure what an entrepreneur does.

"Have you done your pro forma?"

"My what?"

He chuckled, walking me toward their kitchen, "Your business plan. Don't worry, I can help you with it."

That evening, he told me all about business plans, what they should include, and what should go into the research of one.

He worked with me over the next three months. He would ask me something like how much money I thought my company would make. I would give him some figures, but he always wanted more details, so I would go home and continue working.

I remember struggling with the figures until 2:00 AM one morning. I threw down my pencil and said to myself, "I'm done! I can't do this anymore!" Just as I was getting up from my chair, I immediately sat down, picked up my pencil and started back up again. It was as if there were a divine intervention driving me. I was not going to stop.

When you're ready for success in your life, you will need mentors. In this case, I knew how to make flower arrangements, and I had a good idea of how to run a flower shop and how to get loyal customers; what I didn't know was the money side of the business. Greg taught me the hard lessons.

Finally, I had my business plan put together. Greg, went to a bank to secure a business loan for me. But after all my hard work, I was turned down.

When Greg gave me the bad news, I said, "That's okay."

"What?" He asked, surprised.

"It's no big deal. When one door closes, another door opens. I am going to do this thing."

Greg smiled, "I appreciate the enthusiasm, Jerry. Just keep working on your pro forma, and I'll keep working on getting you a loan."

A few weeks later, I negotiated a lease on a building for my flower shop, and got my business license. The only thing missing was money.

A positive attitude is important in success, but that doesn't mean things will be easy. I had every confidence I would be able to open my business, and I moved forward with that expectation. But money didn't just come to me; I had to keep working. And I have to tell you, I got discouraged. I worried at times that all my efforts would be for nothing. But at the end of the day, I knew I would find the money and have my shop.

One day, I found a man willing to loan me $35,000. His terms were 12% interest and a third of my business. Before I agreed, I asked Greg about the loan. His advice? Don't take the money.

I was crushed. I was so close to getting my business started. And yet I trusted my mentor. He told me my company could be worth a lot of money, so I shouldn't give it away in the beginning.

But how could my company be successful if it never got off the ground? My previous enthusiasm was drained.

Later in the week, Greg called me back. "Jerry, what is your projected electric bill per month for your new lease?"

I looked at my phone with exhaustion and replied, "I have no fucking idea."

Greg was silent for a moment. "Jerry come over to my office tomorrow, and we will talk."

When I arrived at Greg's office, I sank into a chair across from him. I figured that we were going to go over my business plan again, so I slid my latest copy across his desk.

Greg pushed it aside and asked, "How much money do you need to open your business?"

"$15,000." I knew the figure because I had struggled over and over to see if there were anyway I could start my business for less money.

"Jerry, this is what I am going to do. I am going to lend it to you myself, and it's going to be $20,000 because you need some extra. The only thing I ask is your word that if your business goes belly-up, you will still get the money back to me. And I want 15% interest amortized over 24 months from the day I give you the money."

I smiled broadly. The terms didn't bother me. I knew my business would be successful. I thanked him deeply.

"I'll have the check for you tomorrow. What time do you want to come over?"

"What time do you open?"

Greg laughed. "I'll see you in the morning then."

From there, our business relationship started. I kept to the terms, paying off his loan on schedule. And in the process, we developed a friendship.

Greg and Yvonne became close friends of mine. They asked me to be godfather to their children. I graciously accepted the honor. I took the relationship seriously by helping to raise the boys. At times, I was able to help build and maintain the relationships between the boys and their father, especially through their adolescent years. As they grew up, I mentored them, giving back in part what their father gave to me. Today, the boys are adults and they still view me as their second father.

The important things in life don't come easy. If you want to be successful you have to put in the hard work. Often, that work is not simply grinding through daily routines; you will probably have to do the research, and the numbers, and even grind through forms. But if you keep your eye on your goals, and work toward them, not only will success come to you, but people will also enter your life to help you when you need them most.

CHAPTER 6

Opening My Own Shop

When I opened up my flower shop in 1988, I chose a space directly across the street from a flower shop that had been established seven years prior. Most people would question my decision; they would believe I should have set up shop a distance away from competition.

I never worried about competition. I believed that the space I chose for my business was the best place for a flower shop, and I believe that if you take care of your business, your business will take care of you. Your competition might as well be nearby because then you will succeed in front of them.

Of course, it wasn't that easy opening a flower shop. As it turned out, I was starting a new business in a market that was just then changing.

People were beginning to buy their flowers from grocery stores. Major supermarkets were opening their own flower departments. Back then, supermarkets didn't have florists; they just offered cut flowers and a few minimal arrangements.

The supermarket entry into the flower business had a big impact on the floral industry. Small shops tried to compete by lowering their prices. The problem was that they didn't have the buying power of the major chains, nor the healthy margins.

So how did I expect to compete against the supermarkets and the shop across the street? By differentiating myself. I was determined to give people a reason to bypass grocery stores and other flower shops, and come specifically to me.

While most flower shops were trying to compete with grocery stores and lower their prices, I raised mine. When a grocery store or the guy across the street was selling a dozen roses for $35, my rose bouquets were $75 to $125. I didn't try to trim my margin; instead, I enhanced the quality of my arrangements.

What I knew was that if a guy wanted to impress his girlfriend or wife, he wouldn't settle for the cheapest; he'd gladly go after the $125 arrangement. You see, I didn't simply smash twelve roses together, I excelled in exceptional designs. With my bouquets, a man could overwhelm a woman.

When he walked into my flower shop, I'd ask him, "Do you want to make her the envy of the office, and have all the other women talk about how great her boyfriend or husband is? This is what you want to do…"

Those customers returned the next day to thank me. Why? Because you can't buy the feeling you get when your wife or girlfriend is overjoyed by the flowers you sent, by how she feels when she is the envy of the office. What man wouldn't pay a few extra dollars to show his love in that way?

If you take care of your clients, they will love spending their money with you. This doesn't happen until you feel the obligation to carry the finest quality products and deliver the best customer service. More important, you must maintain relationships with your customers.

In business, and in life, you want to differentiate yourself from others. You don't do this on price, but on the quality you bring to your business and your life. When others are trying to cut prices, services, and quality, make sure you exceed expectations, that you are diligent, and you return phone calls. Make sure your customers know that you are someone they can rely on. When you differentiate yourself in these ways, people will bypass cheaper competitors and work directly with you.

CHAPTER 7

THE RICH GET RICHER

Because I was the youngest florist in the industry in Northern California, I was able to distinguish myself from the competition by doing what my competitors didn't do.

For instance, if a bride-to-be called to schedule a consultation. I would ask her a few questions to find out if she was shopping around. If she was, I'd suggest she visit the other shops first. That way she wouldn't have to visit my shop twice. I would, however, give her pricing over the phone, something my competitors would not do, so that she would have something to compare to as she visited the other shops. My motto is that if you are more "informational" rather than "promotional," people will see you as an expert in your field.

Before I knew it, I was booking 125 weddings a year. Soon I was the most successful florist in the area.

I became so successful that I began to worry about continuing to grow my business. I racked my brain, and realized there are other professionals in the wedding industry: photographers, bakers, caterers, and so on. How do I get these places to promote Jerry's Flowers?

I came up with the idea of creating my own group of professionals called "Your Wedding Portfolio." It had a photographer, caterer, a place to hold the wedding, and of course, my flower shop. I called the different companies I wanted in the portfolio, and said, "I would like to include you in my very exclusive group of wedding professionals."

I charged them $500 a piece to make sure they were committed to the program. We met once a month at a mansion that had been converted into a bed and breakfast, in Walnut Creek. (They were one of my fifteen merchants included in my wedding portfolio.) We would talk about how we could market ourselves.

By promoting each other, we all got business. Instead of paying hundreds for an ad in the newspaper, we would all pitch in, say, $30. When the wedding shows came around, I would go to the promoter and negotiate for a bigger booth. Our competitors would pay between $500 and $1,000 for their booth, while we shared ours. Where the promoter was originally getting $1,000 for a booth, we were paying $1,500, leaving the promoter feeling like she made a deal. In fact, by consolidating 14 vendors into one booth, she was losing out on the additional revenue. But we were minimizing our cost of doing business.

This is why the rich keep getting richer; they know that the upper echelon of professionals in an industry support one another. And when they do, they all succeed. It's better to partner than to fight it out.

The Rich get Richer

Me as a young man dreaming of what it would be like to be part of Hollywood.

My Life on the Red Carpet

CHAPTER 8

MEETING OPRAH WINFREY

A few years ago, Oprah Winfrey threw a wedding for her trainer, Bob Greene, at her estate in Montecito, CA. One of my best friends, Michael Holmstrom, owns Signature Valet, and has organized valet and parking services for all of her events.

When I learned about the wedding, I asked Michael if he needed help with the event.

"Sure. You can be the suit." He meant that I could be the person who greeted guests coming to the wedding.

On Friday, the day before the wedding, I drove down to Montecito. Mine was the only car that was allowed on Oprah's property. When I drove up to her gate, the security guard knew who I was. I did, however, have to sign a confidentiality agreement to park on the property.

I caught a glimpse of Oprah that day. She was about 30 feet away with her dog.

The valets arrived shortly after I did to be debriefed. During the talk, Stedman Graham came out and said hello to everyone. He shook every valet's hand, which I thought was very gracious of him.

On Saturday, the guests had to park off property and be shuttled to the front of the house where the wedding was held. Then after the wedding, people were shuttled around the mansion to the backyard where the reception was held. Back there, they had a humongous tent. It was as big as a house. It had a dance floor, stage, the whole works.

Of course the party went late into the night, and most of the guests were invited to stay over. After all, this was a two-day event.

The next day, the guests were treated to a glorious Sunday brunch. Of course I was there.

And that's when I met Oprah. She was walking with her mother over the grass, with her shoes in hand.

I took advantage of the opportunity to walk over to her. I touched her arm. "Excuse me, Mrs. Winfrey. You are the most gracious host. And I thought it was important for you to know that on Friday, Stedman shook every valet's hand, and introduced himself. They were so taken aback that even today they are talking about it."

She was pleased that I shared that story with her.

Later, after getting into the SUV that would take her around to the front of the house (the estate is that large), she leaned out the window and asked, "What is your name again?"

"Jerry Olivarez."

She put her hands to her chest, and said "Thank you very much. I will see you again."

I thought, "How are we ever going to see each other again?"

Well, I did see her again.

In 2010, I was working with the Jackson family. I was at their Havenhurst Estate in California when I asked Katherine Jackson, "Would you consider having an interview with Oprah Winfrey?"

Katherine informed me of some personal reasons for why she didn't feel comfortable giving the interview.

I said, "Mrs. Jackson, thank you for enlightening me. You won't hear anything from me about this again."

Then, from across the room, Joe Jackson said, "Jerry if that interview happens, I will walk from Las Vegas to L.A. to see it myself."

I smiled.

My Life on the Red Carpet

Later, when Katherine Jackson's book came out, her publishing company set up a world-exclusive interview with Oprah.

The interview was to be shot at the Jackson Family Havenhurst Estate in Encino, California. I was in New York at the time, but I flew to Southern California for the interview.

In the library with Mrs. Jackson and Mr. Jackson.

When Oprah arrived, she introduced herself to everybody in the room. When she greeted me, I reminded her of what I had said about Stedman at Bob Greene's wedding.

She looked into my eyes and listened to everything I said. She was present in the moment, and made me feel comfortable sharing with her.

There was an entire camera crew there, plus a behind the scenes crew. I didn't know there was a documentary being filmed. I thought they were all part of the same show.

As we prepared for the interview, I helped Joe Jackson with his necklace. He was excited and proud about the interview.

I whispered to him, "Mr. Jackson, had I known you were going to be here, I would have brought you a comfortable pair of walking shoes."

He looked at me and we both smiled, remembering his earlier statement.

After the interview we had a dinner, after which I presented Oprah with a Michael Jackson commemorative belt. She loved it, and put it on. "You mean I can have this? This is my belt?"

I said, "Yes. And I have another gift for you."

An artist I had been working with, Jorge Burtin, knew of my affinity for Oprah and gave me a beautiful pixaic of Oprah's eyes. He titled it "The Dancer." A pixaic is made of thousands of pieces of glass. When I knew I was going to be meeting Oprah at Katherine Jackson's home at the Havenhurst Estate, I called Jorge and asked him if he would mind if I gave Oprah the pixaic he'd given to me.

He said "Of course. Give it to her."

So after I presented her with the belt, I said, "I'd like to draw your attention to this side of the room. A friend of mine is an artist, and he knew of my admiration of you. He gave me this pixaic of you. When I knew I was coming to see you, I asked him if he would mind if I gifted it to you on behalf of myself, Katherine Jackson, and Joe Jackson. He agreed, so I would like to present this to you.

When I unveiled it, she loved it. "Oh my God, who did this?"

Oprah wearing the Michael Jackson Commemorative Belt

"Jorge Burtin. He titled it 'The Dancer.'"
"Those are my eyes," she exclaimed.
"Yes, Mrs. Winfrey."

The point of my experiences with Oprah is that when you think it, wish it, imagine it, and accept it as something that has already happened, the wheels get in motion. You will truly achieve what you believe in. It is the power of positive thinking, accepting, and being grateful as if you've already achieved it. Then, you are allowing the universe to manifest your vision.

Be aware of your thoughts. Your mind can be like a runaway steam train if you let it. It can take you off to the bad

Simon and Oprah Winfrey at Katherine Jackson's Havenhurst home where Michael grew up.

events of the past and push fearful thoughts of the future. Those out of control thoughts are creating your future.

How do you become aware of your thoughts? One way is to stop, and ask, "What am I thinking right now? What am I feeling right now?" The moment you ask, you are aware because you have brought your mind back to the present moment.

Do this a hundred times each day because all of your powers are in your awareness of now. I tell myself to become more aware, to remember to remember. I ask the universe to give me a gentle nudge, to bring me back to the present whenever my mind is taken over and is having a party at my expense.

That gentle nudge happens when I bump something or drop something, or when there is a loud noise. All these are signals that I need to bring my mind back to the present.

Jorge Burtin's pixaic "The Dancer"

When I hear these signals, I stop immediately and ask myself, "What am I thinking? What am I feeling?"

In the moment I do that, I am aware. The very moment you ask yourself if you are aware, you are aware.

When you are thinking you are having a bad day, or that things aren't going in the right direction, stop. Say, "This is okay. Let me change my train of thought so I can feel better, so I can open up to the universe, so that I can bring more greatness into my life."

Months after presenting the commemorative belt and pixaic, I saw myself on television. I didn't know it at the time, but the extra cameras at the interview were filming for a documentary for Oprah's *OWN* network. The moment

Oprah receiving "The Dancer" that I just gave her.

the show aired, my phone began ringing with people telling me they had seen me with Oprah. In a sense, I was on the *Oprah Winfrey Show*. And that was beyond my wildest dreams.

CHAPTER 9

GO TO THE TOP

There are many relationships in business. Yes, your customers are the most important, but you have to also pay attention to vendors and other businesses that support yours.

For instance, FTD is an important company for florists. When a florist is an FTD member, they can extend their business by taking local orders for deliveries in other parts of the world. Similarly, if someone somewhere else in the world wants to send flowers to someone in your community, you can get that order.

It works like this: When someone walks into your store and wants to send an arrangement to New York, they give you the order. You give FTD that order. They give it to a florist in New York. The New York florist bills FTD, who then bills you.

The logo is known worldwide, so they have strenuous requirements for florists in their network. For instance, you have to have been in business for a year before you can apply, and must pass their strenuous inspection and criteria.

I knew who the local FTD representative was because I'd been in the floral industry for many years. I would often see him around town.

When my business had been in operation for a year, I saw him eating lunch with a competing florist. I walked up to his table and announced that I wanted to be an FTD florist. "That's great, Jerry," he said. "I'll send you a brochure."

To me, that was a slap in the face. I wanted to carry their logo, and all he would do was send me a brochure. So I called FTD directly, and they also sent me a brochure, which frustrated me further.

When I ran into the FTD representative a few months later, I tried again. "What do I need to do to be an FTD florist?" I asked him.

"I'll call you," he said, but he never did. Worse, he didn't send me anything, not even the brochure.

I would continue to see him having lunch with other florists. Each time I approached him about the application process, he'd blow me off.

One day it dawned on me; if I become an FTD florist it would mean that the incoming orders in this area would be split with one more guy. So the pie would be cut with an extra piece. The other florists having lunch with the representative didn't want me to be an FTD florist. They were making sure my application didn't get started.

When you don't get what you want locally, go to the top. I called Champaign, Illinois and asked for the president of FTD. The gatekeeper took my name and promised that the president would call me back.

Later that day I received the call. Now for a florist, getting a call from the president of FTD is like getting a call from the President of the United States.

Undaunted, I told him I was a second generation florist, and I described my exceptional flower shop. I also informed him that I had contacted the FTD representative in Northern California. "Every time I run into him, he just sends me a brochure. The last time I saw him, he was having lunch with four or five local florists, and I realized there might be politics involved."

"Perhaps," I concluded, "It's because I'm 27 years old, and the youngest florist in Northern California."

"Jerry," the president replied, "I understand exactly what you are saying. I am 42 years old, and I am the youngest president FTD has ever had. I have fought the politics myself. If you are still willing to be an FTD florist, I will have someone in your office in two hours."

It was only 45 minutes before the FTD representative was in my office, looking like a beaten puppy. The representative said, "Jerry, I just got a call from the president of FTD."

"Steve," I said, "This is nothing personal. I just want to be an FTD florist."

He nodded. "Okay, let me look around."

The man spent two hours grading me. He made sure I had the proper number of blooming plants, green plants, and varieties of roses, cut flowers, and displays. He watched my father make arrangements in the back room.

Finally, he came back to where I was working. "Let me tell you something, I have filled out literally hundreds of these applications, and I have never graded any flower shop superior in every category. You should be proud that you have achieved a superior rating in all categories. I apologize that it has taken me so long to get here. If you just sign here, you will be an FTD florist."

I was amazed at how humble he was, given the circumstances. His attitude showed me that he knew that my going to the top was not personal. He understood that I was doing what needed to be done for my business.

Don't let people get in your way. Politics and personal interests will often work against you. When this happens, go to the top. Let everyone know it isn't personal; it's business. You are working toward your business goals, and they either need to help you or get out of the way.

CHAPTER 10

MEETING CAROL BURNETT

You may be too young to remember Carol Burnett, but she had one of the best variety shows on television. She made America laugh on Saturday nights from 1967 to 1978.

When Ted Mann passed, I attended his funeral in Beverly Hills out of respect and support for my employer at the time, Johnny Brenden, Mr. Mann's grandson. Mr. Mann was a businessman best known for the Mann's Chinese Theatre on Hollywood Boulevard.

I was staying at the Four Seasons Hotel on Doheny in Beverly Hills. Industry people and celebrities meet in hotels like the Four Seasons, which is secluded yet close to everything. Celebrities feel comfortable there because everyone knows each other, and they won't get mobbed by fans like they do at restaurants.

When I walked into the lobby, Carol Burnett was in the lobby talking with Morgan Freeman.

When she was done with her conversation, I walked up to her and said, "Mrs. Burnett, I wanted to introduce myself. I'm Jerry Olivarez, Johnny Brenden's publicist. I'm in town for Ted Mann's funeral."

She said, "Oh, I read about it in the newspaper."

"I wanted to thank you for all the years of entertainment you brought to my family and other families in America."

She said, "Thank you very much. And what was your name again?"

I told her, and she smiled as we went our separate ways.

About an hour later, I was outside of the Four Seasons, waiting for my car. At that moment, Carol Burnett walked out of the hotel with her daughter. When she saw me, she turned to me and said, "Oh Jerry, this is my daughter."

What I thought was so fascinating was that not only did Carol Burnett remember my name, but she took the extra effort to introduce me to her daughter.

It is important to remember people's names. The simple courtesy of calling them by their name and introducing them to someone else will endear you to them, and get you further in life.

CHAPTER 11

DAVID AND GOLIATH

Back in 1989, having an 800 phone number was a big deal for a company. I purchased one for my flower shop when I was accepted by FTD. That number went out to 25,000 florists around the world.

Back then you didn't own your phone number. So when I "bought" my number from MCI, I was essentially leasing it.

When AT&T began selling numbers at a lower price, it made sense for me to switch companies. Switching phone companies was a big deal back then. Your contract had to run out on your number and then you would switch companies and get a new number. You then had to make sure everyone knew your new number. Without email or websites to notify people of the change, it took a lot of planning and work.

I told MCI that I wanted to drop their number at the end of April. And I told AT&T that I wanted their number up and running on May 1st. I had my secretary check a couple of weeks prior to the end of April to make sure everything was in place. All the papers were signed and everything looked good.

But it wasn't. The new number didn't work on Saturday, May 1st. And since it was the weekend, and there wasn't customer service until Monday, I had to wait.

On Monday, AT&T assured me that the number would be working within the next couple of days. And yet, three days later, it still wasn't up. I called again, and listened to similar assurances, and still nothing happened.

Mother's Day was coming up, a very important day in the flower business. The money florists make on this holiday gets them through the slower months of summer.

Unfortunately, AT&T didn't get my number up in time, and I lost a lot of revenue during the almost two weeks that I didn't have a phone. Who knows how many orders would have come through in those weeks leading up to Mother's Day.

So I called AT&T again, and said, "My number wasn't up until after the Mother's Day holiday. During that time, I lost a lot of business, and I need to talk with someone." They connected me to their legal department, who told me that the phone company is governed by a tariff law; therefore, they don't have to reimburse for any loss of business due to interruption of service. If they had to pay for business lost every time a line went down, they'd be paying out millions of dollars a year.

He said respectfully, "Don't try to fight us. Our lawyers are on retainers. You wouldn't win."

I asked, "Could you please send me a copy of that tariff law. I've never heard of it."

"Sure. I'll fax it to you."

At that time, the paper in fax machines was on rolls. As the fax started coming over the phone line, the paper began to spool out. It didn't end until I had five feet of paper in front of me. I looked at it. Sure enough, in the first paragraph on the first page, it said that AT&T is governed by a tariff law. If a number goes down, they are not responsible for lost income. That is all I needed to read. The reality was, my number did not go down; they had solicited my business, and had assured me that there would not be an interruption in my service when I switched from MCI.

So I picked up the phone, and began trying to get a hold of the executive officers of AT&T. I finally reached a nice administrative assistant to the president. I explained what the situation was, and what their lack of follow-through on their business promise had cost my business, especially since the gap in service came before the biggest business day of the year for a florist.

The lady listened to me, and then said, "Jerry, this is very important to us. Did you have an 800 number last year?"

"Yes, with MCI."

"Send me over your bills, and I'll see what I can do."

Within minutes, she received a fax with my information.

She called me about a week later, asking questions like, "What does it cost to make a flower arrangement? What percentage of your annual business happens during the first two weeks of May? What is your profit margin on an arrangement? When your phone rings, what is the percentage of deals that are closed?"

After we talked back and forth, I wasn't sure where we were headed. She thanked me for my answers.

She called me back later that day, and told me that there were a lot of 800 number calls around Mothers Day the year before. She wanted to confirm that I closed about 80% of those calls, and that my average order was $50. I told her that she was correct in her figures. She thanked me again and hung up.

Two weeks later, I received a plain envelope. I might have thrown it away, but fortunately I open all of my mail. Inside was a check for over $7,000. While that money represented what I would have made after expenses, there wasn't any labor involved in generating that $7,000, except for my phone calls. So, it turned out to be a very profitable Mother's Day after all.

There are certain ways to communicate with vendors, and there are ways to present your case without threatening or becoming upset. When we are polite and persistent, people will want to help us. I could have been angry with AT&T. I could have threatened, whined, and complained. But I was polite in how I presented myself, and they went out of their way to help. When you treat people with respect, they feel good about helping you.

Don't feel intimidated if you are the underdog. Even with five feet of paper supposedly supporting them, they were still wrong. Read the details, and examine the fine print. Know your case, and present it well. Some people feel strong when they believe they have power over you, but they usually want to do the right thing.

Finally, don't listen to what other people tell you. If you are right, pursue it. If I had listened to the attorneys, I would never have gotten that $7,000 check, and who knows what would have happened to my business that year. And if that year had not been successful, who knows how my life would have turned out. It was worth the effort.

CHAPTER 12

THE *YELLOW PAGES*

Speaking of telephone companies, in the old days, they distributed a book called the *Yellow Pages*. This was a listing of local businesses and their phone numbers. If you wanted, say, a flower shop, you would look up florist in the *Yellow Pages* and find a listing of all the nearby flower shops.

In the late 1980s and the 1990s, I needed to advertise in the *Yellow Pages* to get customers. The *Yellow Pages*, back then, was an important place for an advertisement for flower shops. An ad in the *Pacific Bell Smart Yellow Pages* was $14,000. For that money, I was to receive a large ad telling potential customers what I had to offer. This was a significant investment, but the money spent on a large ad would mean that my ad was earlier in the listing and much more visible to potential customers. A small ad would have been a mere expense for my business, but I chose, instead, to make an investment for a larger ad that would yield a greater return.

But when the *Yellow Pages* came out, my ad was not in the book. I checked all the appropriate pages, but didn't find any mention of my flower shop. So I called Pacific Bell to ask about my ad.

After some searching, they discovered that they had put my ad in the *East Contra Costa Yellow Pages*, instead of the *Central Contra Costa County Yellow Pages*. Well, East Contra Costa County was two cities away from me.

"That isn't going to do me any good," I explained. Their mistake could put me out of business.

Their solution was to give me an ad at half price the next year, in the *Central Contra Costa Yellow Pages*.

"How will that help me if I'm out of business?" I asked.

Their answer? Give it to me for free the next year.

"You're not hearing me." I said, "I need something right now to keep me in business so that I will be around to advertise with you next year."

Without a lawyer, I negotiated with them. You see, the *Yellow Pages* bills you once a month, but only prints the book one time per year. So, I hadn't actually made a payment at this point. The fact was that now I needed $14,000 from them so that I could use it for other advertising to keep my business going. Combining their $14,000 with the $14,000 I had earmarked for the large ad would enable me to keep my head above water for the coming year. After communicating with the company for two weeks, they called to inform me that they would cut me a check for $14,000.

When I arrived at the San Francisco offices to pick up the check, they told me they had never written a check out to someone like this before. They went on to tell me this was solely due to my excellent communication skills.

The point is, I was once again in a poor negotiating position. They were the big company, I was the small flower shop owner. I let them know that they had the power to put me out of business. I didn't threaten them; instead, I gave them the decision over my business. And then I presented my case in a reasonable, respectful manner.

CHAPTER 13

GETTING THE STORY CORRECTED

My flower shop was in a building that also had a dry cleaner, a convenience store, and a little restaurant.

One day, there was a fire in the restaurant, and it spread to the adjoining stores. Since the fire was at the other end of the building, my business was safe.

The next day, the story ran in the *Contra Costa Times* that my building had caught fire. They named Jerry's Flowers as one of the businesses that was affected by the fire, so everyone thought I was out of business.

It was a pretty slow week after the fire, so I went down to the newspaper offices, and met with the editor. "You ran this story that my flower shop burned down, and it didn't. You need to print a retraction."

He sat there, staring at me. "We can put a retraction with all the other ones on the back page."

"No. That's not good enough. The retraction needs to have the same exposure as the original article, and should state that my flower shop did not burn and is still open."

He didn't budge. We went back and forth, and I could tell I was wasting my time.

Finally I said, "I tell you what, I'll let Margaret and Dean Lesher know that we need to do something to raise awareness that my business is still operating."

Now, Margaret and Dean were not only friends of mine, they were also the owners of the newspaper. I wasn't disrespecting the editor, nor was I threatening; I only wanted him to know that I did not find his solution acceptable, and that I was willing to do what I thought was necessary to protect my business.

His position changed quickly. "Give me a couple of days. I will get back to you."

Of course, I agreed. When people feel like they have the power to do something positive for you, they will get creative.

In this case, the editor decided to run a follow-up story on the front page about the fire. He let the readers know that my shop was not affected by the fire.

What more could I ask for? I was on the front page of the newspaper. The continuing story of the fire drew a lot of attention. And as people read, they learned that I was still open for business.

You see, when you present your case well, and when you are respectful, you don't need to get attorneys involved, nor do you have to cave to the powerful people. By giving them the power, you will get what you want.

CHAPTER 14

MEETING JOHNNY BRENDEN

I built my business through relationships. I didn't sit by the phone waiting for people to come to me; I went to them.

One of my strategies was to move through town handing out my card. When I would see people who I believed would appreciate the quality of the arrangements I created, I would respectfully approach them, give them my card, and ask them to visit my shop.

I often saw Johnny Brenden at different restaurants around Walnut Creek. He has a look that is difficult to miss, plus he always had a gorgeous woman on his arm.

I walked up to Johnny one time, introduced myself, and complimented him, "Every time I see you, you're always with a drop-dead gorgeous woman."

Johnny smiled. "Thanks."

Later that evening, he came over to my table and introduced himself. "I'm Johnny Brenden. I own Brenden Theatres." He handed me his card. "You should come visit sometime."

At that moment I thought, "This guy is out of my league. We are worlds apart. There isn't anything I could do for him beyond making wonderful arrangements for the beautiful women in his life." We all have insecurities, and I certainly have mine.

When Johnny's father passed, Johnny was raised by his grandfather, Ted Mann, and grandmother, Rhonda Fleming, a famous Golden Age movie star who starred with the likes of Ronald Reagan and Bing Crosby.

Growing up in this household taught Johnny the movie business, both from the actor's view and the theater owner's. As an adult, Johnny began opening theaters in Northern California.

Just knowing who Johnny was and what he had already accomplished at that point is his life caused me to resist his invitations. But every time he saw me around town, he would invite me again.

Finally, after a few months of running into him, I took Johnny up on his invitation.

On the arranged day, I drove to Pittsburgh, CA. Johnny's secretary was like a real-life Barbie Doll with big blonde hair, hot pink lips with matching fingernail polish—a true bombshell.

"I'm here to see Mr. Brenden," I announced.

"Oh, I'll go get him."

When she returned with Johnny, he was wearing ripped jeans, tennis shoes, and a stylish t-shirt. He greeted me and enthusiastically grabbed my wrist and walked me into the largest movie theater I'd ever seen.

"I want you to advertise on this screen," he said.

"I can't afford that kind of advertising, sir."

"No, I want to give you this advertising. All I ask is that you send an arrangement of flowers for me on occasion. I promise I won't take advantage. But, I will only do this if you put your picture on the ads."

At that time, I didn't know why he wanted me to have my picture on the screen, but I agreed. About a month later, after my ad had gone up, people began enthusiastically approaching me to say they had seen my advertisement at the theater. They came up to me at the grocery store, restaurants, and the mall. I would gladly give them my business card. Most of these people would eventually call me when they needed flowers. After all, it's nice to deal with the owner directly.

You see, Johnny's theater was ahead of its time. There was nothing else like it in the area. He knew what he was doing. He knew people would see my face and recognize me later. It was the best advertising I had ever done.

In fact, after I started working for Johnny years later, I began selling the on-screen advertising for his company and continued to use the same M.O. I told realtors and other companies to put their pictures on the screen. It certainly adds to one's ego when people tell them they have seen their picture on the big screen. It's like being a local celebrity.

Back at the theater, I thanked Johnny for his offer and hospitality. Thinking our business was concluded, I moved to the door.

"Where are you going?" he asked.

"I'm sorry. I thought we were done."

"Come on, I have something to show you," he said.

We walked out the front of the theater to where Johnny's fire-engine red corvette was parked on the sidewalk in front of the theater. "Follow me to my warehouse," he said.

We drove a few blocks to the building. Johnny walked me inside. The front section was set up like an office, but behind some doors stretched about 5,000 square feet of space.

Johnny shared with me his plans for the space, "A kitchen is going here, a bathroom over there. All in black marble. A sauna and steam room over there. And a loft. Along the back wall will be a huge screen and a $250,000 sound system."

As I listened, I thought it would take years to create Johnny's vision, but he had it all done in two weeks.

After touring the space, I said, "This is really cool Johnny. I'll see you later."

"Where are you going?"

"Well, I'm going home," I said.

"No. Don't go. Follow me."

"Follow you where?"

"Back to my house."

It felt rude to turn him down; after all, he'd been such a great host, and I enjoyed spending time with him.

So I followed him to Walnut Creek. We pulled into a condo complex. The building was nice, but I was surprised when I walked into Johnny's unit. The floors were black and white checkered. The walls and ceiling were all done in foil. There was a huge fish tank in the living room, the likes of which I hadn't seen before.

With Johnny Brenden

Within a few minutes of being there, a buddy of his showed up at the condo.

After meeting the friend, I said, "Thanks, Johnny. I'll see you later."

"Where are you going?" he asked.

"Johnny, you have plans. I'll see you later."

"No. Don't leave."

"Johnny, I gotta go."

"Come on. We're going to the city. I've got a limo waiting for us outside."

The next thing I knew, I was in a limo headed into San Francisco. I spent most of the day with Johnny and I was given a glimpse of what his life is like. Johnny showed me one of the best days of my life.

As our friendship deepened, Johnny often took me to lunch and dinner, and invited me on little excursions. Even when I offered to pay my share, he'd pick up the tab.

I felt guilty for all the money Johnny was spending on me. I brought it up during lunch one day. I said, "You know, Johnny, I appreciate all this, but I wasn't born with a silver spoon in my mouth…"

His hand slapped the table. "Let me clarify something for you. It was a 24 karat gold spoon in my mouth. Jerry, don't ever try to compete with me because you can't."

He wasn't trying to demean me, and I understood that. Someone else might have been offended by this comment, but I got it. What he wanted to do was set the stage. He was putting me at ease, and letting me know that he wouldn't be thinking I was freeloading when we were out. Also, he didn't want to run the risk that I wouldn't go out with him because I couldn't afford it.

I know this now, because I, too, like to include others in the things I enjoy doing. I let them know I'll take care of it so they won't worry about it. They do me the honor of having their company. At the end of the day, it's about including rather than excluding, and giving other people the opportunity to share experiences with you.

My Life on the Red Carpet

CHAPTER 15

DRESS FOR SUCCESS

I received a call a few months after meeting Johnny. "Hi, this is Johnny Brenden's executive assistant."

"Yes?"

"Johnny needs you to go shopping with him today to buy some furniture."

"Yeah, sure," I said, confused.

"Okay. He'll be picking you up in 45 minutes. He wants you to be wearing a double-breasted suit. And have your attaché case."

I looked at my phone, thinking, "Are you kidding?" Of course I agreed, but it seemed like an odd request.

I've always worn suits, and when Johnny met me I had a gold Haliburton attaché case. I've since learned that how I dress elevated Johnny. He can show up in $800 ripped jeans and $100 t-shirts with me standing near him in my suit and holding my case. People assume I'm the one holding his money. In Hollywood, if you surround yourself with people who look like executives, the perception is that you are important.

For instance, before they built the Palms Casino Resort in Las Vegas, and before I was working for Johnny, he asked me to come visit him in his office.

I sat down across from Johnny and we started talking about nothing in particular. In the middle of our conversation, people began coming into the office and gathering at the conference table.

I started to stand. "Okay, I'll see you later."

Johnny motioned me to sit back down. "No. Stay there. Just stay there."

He got up and went over to the table where George Maloof, the man behind the Palms Casino Resort, sat with his lawyers.

Meanwhile, I'm just sitting there at Johnny's desk, not sure what to do. I'm thinking, "These guys are discussing deals worth tens of millions of dollars. I shouldn't be here."

Then I realized Johnny wanted me sitting there. He wanted Mr. Maloof, his attorneys, and the other executives to wonder about the guy at his desk.

People judge us by how we dress. I have had many opportunities come my way because I wear suits. I don't look like a humble florist, so people treat me differently.

As they say, "The clothes make the man."

Dress for Success

CHAPTER 16

NEXT STEPS

In 1994, I merged my flower business with Jory's flowers. I was doing very well and wanted to take my business to the next level. To do that, I needed an infusion of cash.

The floral industry is time consuming, and I needed time to focus on other business deals. The result was that I wasn't minding the store. A flower shop doesn't do as well when the owner isn't there.

Worse, I couldn't afford health insurance. I felt fine, but my blood pressure was high. And since I couldn't afford the medication, I stopped taking it.

One day I went for a bike ride. Afterward, I sat down and everything started going away from me, almost like a tunnel.

I called 911.

The fire department gave me nitroglycerin and took me to the hospital. After being looked over, the doctor said I had suffered a myocardial infarction.

I was shaken. When I went to sleep that night, I had a dream that told me to sell my flower shop. It was clear that I needed to call Donald Hotton and merge with him. A lot of my major decisions in life come from dreams.

When I got to work the next day, the first thing I did was call Donald and invite him to lunch.

He jokingly asked, "Is this going to make me a lot of money?"

"Yes. I'm going to merge my flower shop with yours, and I'm going to double your business in 12 months." This was a bold statement because he had a well established business.

A few weeks after we finished negotiations and the companies merged, I was driving around town. I saw a lot of employees standing outside of a competing flower shop.

My first thought was that it was unusual. So, I parked my car and went inside. I saw two women sitting and asked them if the store was open.

One of the women said, "No. We are with the IRS, and this store has been closed."

I then asked if it was possible that I could buy the shop's phone number.

She replied, "How much?"

"$150?"

"No, you'll have to do better than that."

I told her I'd return in an hour with a cashiers check for $500, which she gladly accepted.

In the 1980s and 1990s, the phone number was the life blood of a flower shop. People might not walk by your shop, but they will pick up the phone and call.

Two hours later, I had purchased the phone numbers of five flower shops that the IRS was shutting down. That quick investment instantly doubled Jory's Flower's business, which is what I had promised.

When you have a conviction, and follow through on your promises, opportunities will come to you. Since I was so convinced I would double Jory's business, I was open to buying the number when I noticed the people standing outside the shop.

Because the deal was so easily done, I went to other flower shops and bought their phone numbers. Soon we had a bank of operators answering the phones.

From that experience, I went national. I created Global Florist and purchased the phone number 888-400-ROSE.

Then I had an idea for quickly expanding our customer base. I approached Chase Manhattan Bank. It took me three months of calling before I got to the right person. I told her my idea: I would offer customers an $11 discount on their flower orders if they used their Chase Manhattan credit card.

She listened and said, "Let's talk."

When I hadn't heard back from her in three months, I began trying to think of a way to get her attention as well as a phone call.

Finally I sent her a $250 arrangement of roses and orchids, with a card that said, "Please call me. Jerry."

She called me at 7:30 that evening. "I just received your flowers. I apologize that we didn't get back to you sooner. The only problem I have is how I will explain these flowers to my husband."

I flew to New York to put together a very successful campaign, and all it cost me was a flower arrangement.

When the credit card statements went out with a flier advertising the deal, the phones started ringing, and they didn't stop. We generated over $100,000 in revenue, and we didn't even print the fliers that went in the statements. Essentially, the success we were experiencing didn't cost a dime in advertising.

The deal went like this: Every time someone used their Chase credit card to purchase flowers with us, we gave them an $11 discount. The average purchase was $60. There was a $12 transfer fee for the order, so we were bringing in essentially a dollar, plus we kept 20% of the actual order. There was also an additional $6 rebate on every order sent.

Of course, we made more money on larger orders, but if you look at the deal, you can see how easily we made money without putting out any actual costs beyond the labor of answering phones. The florists fulfilling the orders had to put up the costs of their materials, and Chase Manhattan put up the costs of placing the inserts in their statements.

We must listen to our dreams, and pursue our goals. Life will throw us a few curveballs, like a myocardial infarction, but from these experiences new opportunities will come our way.

CHAPTER 17

NEW YORK CITY

Since I was a young man, I have wanted to not only visit New York City, but to actually do business there. But as a florist in the Bay Area, few opportunities presented themselves.

And now I was flying to New York City with an appointment at Chase Manhattan Bank.

Even the first cab ride into the city from the airport was overwhelming. I lost track of the sky as the buildings towered over me, making me feel my insignificance in the metropolis.

After I checked into the Doubletree Hotel on Times Square, I took a cab to Wall Street. I shook my head in wonder that I would be doing business there. It was crazy. The Twin Towers were still standing then, and my appointment was on the 75th floor. As I stood before the towers, looking straight upward, I couldn't see the end of them stretching into the sky.

After my successful meeting, I returned to my hotel room with time to spare. I decided that I would see David Letterman.

There was a long line in front of the theater, and the ticketing process seemed to be a rather arduous one. I decided my time would be better spent in my hotel room on the phone.

I called the Ed Sullivan Theater. When the line was picked up, I greeted the man and said, "My name is Jerry Olivarez, CEO of Global Florist. I'm in town tonight and would like to see David Letterman."

In a heavy New York accent, the guy replied, "What's so special about you."

"I don't have an answer."

After a bit, the man said, with a slight smile in his voice, "Be at the front door at 4:30, and ask for me."

That's exactly what I did. I was given a ticket for the front row of the balcony where I could see everything in the theater. David Hyde Pierce was the guest that afternoon.

I truly enjoyed the experience, and thanked the man who gave me the ticket.

Since filming was over at 6:30, I walked down Broadway.

After a block, a group of about a half dozen security guards walked toward me, shielding Rudy Giuliani. It was an election year, and Mr. Giuliani was greeting people, shaking their hands and smiling.

I got along the edge of the sidewalk where he would pass. As he shook my hand with a hello, I thought, "Wow, seeing David Letterman and meeting Mayor Giuliani in one afternoon...it doesn't get better than that for a first-timer in New York."

That evening, I decided to dine at the Supper Club. As I turned up the block, I was confronted with a bunch of cars and paparazzi.

Since I was dressed in a suit and tie, I fit in. I continued to walk into the press of people, hearing the paparazzi yell, "Naomi. Over here. Over here."

The next thing I know, arms are around me, people are taking pictures with me, and I'm in the midst of super-models. Naomi Campbell was right there. It was unbelievable.

I turned around, and Michael Douglas walked over and shook my hand. I looked over his shoulder and saw Timothy Hutton. Before I could catch my breath, Mark Wahlberg and his entourage came over to me. They were a great group of young men, polite and gracious.

Could it get any better? How about meeting Donald Trump?

Not two minutes later, emerging from his limo was The Donald himself, helping his girlfriend out of the car. Because of my proximity to the crowd, I was able to shake his hand and exchange hellos.

Who would ever believe that in one night I had seen so many important people? I've always wanted to meet Donald Trump, and I've always liked Michael Douglas. And there were scores of other celebrities thrown in for good measure.

I walked directly to a payphone (this was before cell phones), and called Yvonne Warner. I excitedly told her about my day and evening. I said, "I think I'm going to have a heart attack tonight and just die because I would not have been able to plan this any better."

She laughed and congratulated me.

When you dream big, great things will happen.

CHAPTER 18

A Changing Industry

With the great success at Global Florist and our campaign with Chase Manhattan, we were riding high, feeling great. Even though it was my plan, and I had put it together, I was still surprised by its quick success.

I was at a business conference in San Francisco atop the Starlight Room, which had an excellent view of the city. I was conversing with the president of FTD. He turned to me and said, "Jerry, Global Florist is one of the top selling florists at this time. I would like to buy it." Being young and basking in the success of the multiple marketing campaigns that I had put together, I'm embarrassed to say that I was feeling a little full of myself.

I hadn't had a lot of business experience yet. I've since learned that when someone wants to buy, you should consider selling. I turned down the offer back then, and I learned my lesson.

It wasn't long before we had competition. Worse, other banks began to charge us twenty cents for each insertion. While Chase Manhattan honored our agreement, and in fact extended the duration of the agreement, our margins were quickly shrinking on our advertising promotion with the credit card statements.

There were also some conflicts between my business partner and I. Finally, I made the decision that it was time to move on, and I looked for a buyer for our company.

I called a gentleman I had met in Nashville at a convention, and proposed to him that he should buy our company.

I was happy when he said that he did want to buy. So we started negotiations.

When things were getting a little sticky in the negotiations, he said, "Let me ask you a question. Who started Global Florist?"

"I did," I answered.

"Who runs it?"

"I do."

"Who markets it?"

"I do."

"Why am I going to buy it? Why am I going to give all this money to your business associate? I could give you this money and have you work for me."

As it turned out, I had already turned in my 30-day notice to the company.

And just like that, I was headed to my new office at 200 Park Avenue in New York City.

I've learned a lot about business over the years, and I would certainly do things differently now than I did back then. For instance, I should have accepted the first offer to buy; on the other hand things worked out for me. But financially and as far as stress goes, my business partner and I would have been ahead had we accepted the first offer.

Also, notice how important connections are. When we needed a buyer, I knew one. In this case, I did more than find a buyer, I found my next boss and became CEO of Fast Floral Network, a subsidiary of Big Apple Florist.

He realized that I had the qualities he wanted. Instead of buying a company, he saw the importance of bringing quality people into his own company.

Companies are built by people. Purchasing product lines or other companies is a good strategy, but always make sure you have a strong team to support your business.

In this case, he probably would have been competing with me had he not hired me.

The flower business had remained relatively unchanged for generations, and I was a key player in the major changes to the industry.

Local shops no longer service their communities. Now, people buy their flowers on the Internet. They may never walk into a flower shop. It all started with a dream. Without that dream, I would not have merged my shop with Donald's, I would not have been looking for a way to double his business, and I would not have seen the success that all those phone lines could bring.

Without those insights, I wouldn't have had a vision for taking the flower business to the world, which led to my idea for Chase Manhattan, which put me in a position to negotiate with my new boss in New York.

So listen to your dreams, and always look for new opportunities.

CHAPTER 19

CHANGING DIRECTIONS

Johnny Brenden was one of the first people to learn of my decision to accept a position in New York. We were at lunch on day, and I let him know that I was offered the position, but would still be living in the Bay Area. I would be commuting to New York for business and staying at the W Hotel in Manhattan when on the East Coast. I promised not to discuss it again; I just mentioned it out of courtesy.

"Thanks, Jerry. I have to build a few more movie theaters before I can justify bringing you on board."

"Thank you, Johnny. Just know that I am always willing to help you out when you need me."

I should have known how quickly Johnny would work. After all, I'd seen how quickly he'd gotten other things accomplished in the past.

In the meantime, I began working in Manhattan. The company already owned a successful flower shop in Grand

My Life on the Red Carpet

Central Station, and they wanted me to launch something like I did for Global Florist.

The deal was that they'd bring me on for three months. How well I built up the business would determine our contract moving forward. I agreed to the terms and got to work.

I brought major deal after major deal to them, and they shot down every one of them. I began to get frustrated. How was I going to determine my value to this company if they weren't going to let me do my job?

I learned that they had borrowed $100,000 in start-up capital to help me build the company. In the meantime, they were using that money for other purposes. Without the ability to move forward on any deals, I began to lose my enthusiasm for the work.

As long as I wasn't getting anything accomplished in New York, I decided to take a long weekend at home in Pleasant Hill, CA.

The next day, I stopped by Johnny's office to say hello.

After our greeting, Johnny said, "Jerry, I want you to tell our vice president that I want you to be on our payroll and you will be our Bill Hertz. He will know what that means."

I stood there, dumbfounded. He didn't ask how things were going with my other job. It was like he didn't care whether I wanted to leave my current job or not.

"Oh," Johnny said, "Call him BC. He'll like that."

Well, I didn't go see Bruce that day. I might say I didn't think Johnny was serious, but I was probably scared of the opportunity that Johnny was giving me.

I saw Johnny later that day and he called me over. "What did BC say?"

I shrugged.

"What? You haven't told him yet?"

"Are you serious?" I asked.

"Yes. Go tell him I want you on the payroll. I want you to make $30,000 plus 15% of on-screen advertising. And tell him I want you to be our Bill Hertz."

I nodded.

"And Jerry, I want you to go to L.A. Book a flight. I want you to build a relationship with Bill. He will teach you.

I was nervous walking to the VP's office. I knocked on his door.

"Yeah, Jerry?"

I walked inside and said, "Johnny wanted me to come up here to tell you he wants me to be on the payroll. I'm to be the executive director of public relations, and his personal publicist." I then told him the amount Johnny said I would be making. I concluded with, "And he wants me to be our Bill Hertz."

He nodded. "Okay. I get it. Let's make it happen at a meeting tomorrow."

The next day, he and I worked out the details. At the time, on-screen ads were only bringing in $500 a month, which would mean I would only be making $75 in commissions. How was I going to make a living on that, especially after leaving my comfortable job in New York?

But then the expense account came and I found that all of my expenses were being taken care of. I thought, "I can make this work."

Best of all, I got to call my own shots. I only had to answer to Johnny.

Johnny already had a few sales people working for him. The best year they had ever had was $90,000 in ad revenue.

In a short time, I was generating over a million a year in onscreen advertising. I was getting $3,000 more a screen than the national average at the time.

At Brenden, I became known as the seventh multiplex theater of the six Brenden multiplex theaters because I brought in as much money as any one theater.

One thing I have learned over the years, and something I was very successful at when I was selling on-screen advertising, is to always get the money first. Get the money for the full contract up front.

When someone hires you to represent them, or to pitch a product or service, keep in mind their dreams, aspirations, and desires. If you don't get paid up front, and they end up changing their mind down the line, it will be tough to get money after the fact. In the meantime, you've invested a tremendous amount of energy and resources. Suing people for the money takes too much effort and energy. It would be better to get your money up front to begin with, then you will be ahead of the eight ball, not behind it.

CHAPTER 20

A Personal Publicist

Johnny literally took me from here to there overnight. His support allowed me to excel at what I do well. Normally, it would take years to accomplish what I did in the movie theater industry, but Johnny saw in me the qualities that would propel his company, and he gave me the opportunity, encouragement, and support to accomplish what I did.

Besides selling advertising, I was also his personal publicist. I say this humbly, but I elevated him in the presence of other people. There's a cachet to having a personal publicist, especially one who is exclusive to you. Other celebrities have people from an agency who represent them as well as other celebrities, whereas I was an extension of Johnny.

I had the ability to speak to anyone, knowing that I was speaking with the authority of Johnny Brenden.

When you are negotiating for someone else, and you're stuck, you can say, "I'll take this information to my person, and get back to you tomorrow." Of course, I knew what Johnny wanted and didn't want, but the tactic would allow me leverage at a later negotiation.

I also acquired things for Johnny. For instance, when he wanted to go to Aspen for New Years, he turned everything over to me and trusted that I'd get him what he wanted, including lodging at the Little Nell.

It seemed like a simple enough request, but when I called the hotel to make a reservation, they told me they were booked for the next four years.

Jerry Olivarez / Johnny Brenden photo shoot in the Brenden Celebrity Suite

A Personal Publicist

I called Johnny and asked him where else he'd like to go.

"Oh, I forgot to tell you, it's really hard to get in there. I've been trying to get in for years."

"Oh, I get it," I said, "I'll call you back in a couple of hours."

I got back on the phone and spoke with the reservation manager. I let them know I represented Johnny Brenden. I told them who Johnny's grandfather and grandmother were.

At the end of my discussion, he said they were still sold out.

"I understand that," I said. "Would you please put us on the list?"

"Yes, but it's four years long."

I tried one more time, "Can I ask you a question?"

"Sure."

"Would you be offended if I called you back in a couple of weeks to see if anything has changed?"

"Sure. You can call me whenever you want."

The next day I was out with Johnny when the phone rang.

"This is the Little Nell."

"Yes?"

"Would you do me a favor and tell me again who Johnny is and who his grandfather is?"

I explained again.

"Jerry, would you like a mountain view or a city view?"

"A mountain view, please."

And just like that, Johnny was booked at the Little Nell for the next several years.

Please note the demeanor of the way I spoke. I presented myself and empowered the gentleman at the Little Nell. There was humbleness in my tone and he knew I was not trying to throw my weight around, nor was I trying to buy my way in. All of this made an impression on him. It is important to know who your audience is.

CHAPTER 21

MEETING BILL HERTZ

When Johnny gave me the new job, he wanted me to fly to Los Angeles to meet Bill Hertz, his grandfather's publicist. He wanted me to establish a relationship with Mr. Hertz and to learn from him.

So, I flew to L.A. to have lunch with Mr. Hertz. I met him at a steakhouse just off of Hollywood Boulevard. As we walked into the restaurant, the maître d said, "Good to see you Mr. Hertz. I will take you to your table."

In Hollywood, it's all about the table; you never take the first one they offer you. It matters where you're seated.

Many people request a specific table, and if you frequent a restaurant, they generally put a reserved sign on your table. In Mr. Hertz's case, they had a table reserved just for him.

Mr. Hertz was in his seventies at the time. He was dressed to the nines with white hair and glasses. He may have been small in stature, but his spirit was larger than life.

Even at his age, he still went to work every day at Paramount Studios. In fact, at his death, he had worked for over 61 years.

Our lunch lasted for more than an hour, and I learned many things in that hour. We quickly established a deep and personal relationship that spanned the next 12 years. In that time, I learned something very important about Mr. Hertz: He always ordered dessert.

Over the years, I could call Mr. Hertz and tell him what I was doing, how I positioned my client, and the issues I was facing. He'd listen to me, ask how I handled it, and generally would assure me that what I thought about doing was exactly what he would do. It was good to get his reassurance, but more important, to know that Mr. Hertz supported my decisions and actions.

In the last few years of his life, he would call me whenever he needed something in Las Vegas. It was an honor to be able to return the favors he had given to me over the years. It was also a massive endorsement of the relationship I built with him. He had trust in me and the confidence that I would deliver what he needed.

For instance, one year I had Sweet 16 tickets to a college basketball game in Oakland. Mr. Hertz and his wife invited me to the game because the stadium was near my house, but more important, because their son was the coach for one of the teams.

I arranged to have a town car pick us up after the game. Mr. Hertz was 81 at the time.

Now, the Oakland Coliseum looks the same whether you are on one side or the other, and because of that, the driver couldn't find us. He was on one side of the stadium, and we were on the other.

I was frustrated that the driver couldn't find us. After all, Mr. and Mrs. Hertz had been on their feet for hours.

Thirty minutes passed, and Mr. Hertz and his wife were getting tired of standing and waiting.

I walked away to find the driver. Sure enough I found him on the other side of the building. I motioned for him to roll down his window.

He said, "Oh there you are."

I said, "Here's what I need you to do. I need you to turn off the car, and get into the back seat. I'm taking over from here."

Now think about this, who turns over their car to someone else? But I spoke with such calm authority that he knew he had messed things up for an important client.

Once in the driver's seat, I drove around the stadium to pick up the Hertzs.

No questions were asked when I got out of the car to open the doors for them, nor did they question why the driver was in the backseat.

I drove them to their hotel, again acting as the driver, opening their doors and ushering them into the hotel lobby.

When they were safely in the elevator, I returned to the car and handed the keys to the driver. I sat in the passenger's seat and let him drive me to my hotel.

Never let them see you sweat. I was seething and nervous on the inside, but all the others saw was confidence.

When you know what needs to be done, do it, and do it confidently.

At 84, Mr. Hertz was told by his doctors that he needed an operation. If it was successful, it would add 15 years to his life. If it wasn't, things would not be good.

Prior to the operation, Mr. Hertz's emails were more profound and spiritual. I believe he was saying his goodbyes.

After the operation, he got pneumonia, and he passed away within weeks.

I was unable to go to his memorial service, but another executive at Brenden Theatres did attend. When she returned to Las Vegas, she told me that during the service, Hertz's grandson spoke about the lives his grandfather had touched. For instance, he said, "There is an executive in the movie theater circuit who was told to learn from him."

When I heard that, I knew the grandson was speaking about me. Of all the thousands of stories he could have told, it was an honor that he chose mine to share at Mr. Hertz's memorial service.

I appreciate all Mr. Hertz did for me as my mentor, and I've followed his example when I mentor other people.

Being a mentor is a big responsibility, especially if the people you mentor follow every word you say. You need to be very careful with the advice you give out. I let those I mentor know what their options are, but I let them make their own decisions. That way, they cannot come back and say that I told them to do the wrong thing. They also enjoy a sense of accomplishment when they make good decisions.

When I was young, I remember wondering why someone would want to take me under their wing, especially when there wasn't anything in it for them. But now that I'm in a position to help others, I understand. There is a lot of satisfaction in sharing your knowledge and insight. There is also a sense of immortality since someone else will be carrying on the knowledge and experience that you've had in life.

Bill Hertz

My Life on the Red Carpet

CHAPTER 22

MEETING ROBIN LEACH

In the whirlwind that became my life, I never forgot lying on the living room floor as a child, watching *Lifestyles of the Rich and Famous*. Every time I met a new celebrity, or sat in a fancy car, or visited someone's mansion, Robin Leach's voice would ring in my head.

And then I met the man himself.

It was the groundbreaking celebration for the Palms Casino Resort. Robin Leach was seated at the same table as Johnny Brenden and me.

I can remember my giddy excitement. I'd lean over to Johnny and say, "Johnny, It's Robin Leach. Look, he's sitting right there."

"I know, Jerry. Calm down."

I felt as if I had just arrived, and, frankly, I had. My life took on a whole other meaning that day with Robin Leach. His presence demonstrated just how far I had come from being the kid in the humble living room, now sitting at the same table with the man himself.

Today, I am proud to say that Robin is my friend, and our friendship is one of the most important relationships I've developed over the years. He is a wonderful man who has shared so much in life. For all the amazing things he has seen, and the wonderful people he's met, he has the ability to make you feel that you are the most important person.

So, I thank Robin Leach for the joy and wonder he has brought to so many people's lives.

George Maloof, Johnny Brendan, Robin Leach, and me for the Brenden Celebrity Star during the CineVegas Film Festival in 2009. This was a very proud moment for me.

I presented my friend Robin Leach with a Brenden Celebrity Star. This was a very proud moment for me.

CHAPTER 23

PUTTING ON A PREMIERE

While selling on-screen advertising was an important aspect of my work with Brenden Theatres, as Johnny Brenden's personal publicist, I also had a lot of red-carpet responsibilities.

When working red carpets, whether at the Palms Casino Resort in Las Vegas or in Los Angeles, I go down early in the day to see the lay of the land, figure out where the media will be, and note the entrances and exits. I also look at how we will access the red carpet, and where shortcuts might be for arriving at the carpet so that we can get in without bringing attention to ourselves before we are standing on the carpet. This way, when I bring the talent, we already know where we are going to go, and we won't waste time.

I also like to get there before the media arrives. This way, the journalists see a familiar face while they are setting up, and I can build a relationship with them. I make sure they are accommodated, and ask them where they want the barricade to be so they get the best view.

Usually, the photographers are wrangled into a horseshoe. There are papers on the ground that say, "Access Hollywood," "Entertainment Tonight," and so on. This way, I will know where everyone is before the talent arrives.

While they are setting up, photographers will call me over. "Who are you?" they ask. "What are you doing? Who are you bringing?"

I tell them I will be bringing Johnny Brenden onto the carpet. I make sure he will be positioned so each of them can get a picture. I ask them if the angles work for them, and if the barriers are too far away. That way they will remember me when the talent arrives. I want to make sure they are ready to take pictures of the talent.

I also go out of my way to make the photographers feel special. You never want the people behind the barriers to feel less important. You want to be respectful of them.

The reality is, if it wasn't for the people behind the barrier, there wouldn't be a reason for my client to be there. The talent walks the red carpet for the media. If the photographers can't get good photos, they won't get paid. So, I make sure the shots are set up well in advance of the talent walking the red carpet.

Thanks to the good relationships I've created with the media, whenever I need someone covered or interviewed, they will do it for me.

I ran into a hurdle at one of the Twilight world movie premieres. I had to get my credentials before I could get my tickets. The credential place wasn't anywhere near where the tickets were. When I returned, I was told I couldn't pick up the tickets until after 5:00 p.m. I was on the master list with two tickets, as was Johnny. The problem was, Johnny needed to be present to pick up his tickets.

Now I knew Johnny wouldn't be picking up his own tickets. To make matters worse, I also needed to pick up tickets for Stan Lee, the legendary creator of Spider-Man and many Marvel Comic characters. I didn't want to look greedy by asking for tickets for everyone. I approached a representative from Stan Lee's company, POW! Entertainment, and got him working on getting Johnny's tickets.

I went to the ticket area at 5:00 p.m. There were literally hundreds of people lined up for tickets. I went over to Stan's assistant and said, "They aren't letting anyone take tickets unless they are here with ID. Johnny and Stan won't be standing in that line."

He said, "I will take care of this for you." He walked past the head of the line, spoke with a few people, and then returned back to me. "Here you go," he said, handing me the tickets.

"Thank you so much," I replied.

I was able to get the tickets because I already knew Stan's assistant. In Hollywood, you access your resources before you need them. If you can get other people to get what you want for you, it doesn't look like you are asking all the time. Then when you do ask for something yourself, people won't feel like you are always asking for favors.

It got more interesting when my contact at Summit Entertainment (the producers of the film) came to me and asked, "How did you get your credentials for the red carpet?"

"What do you mean?" I replied. "I just did."

"Could you do me a favor?" he continued. "Can you get my group of eight people in?"

Now mind you, this was the premiere of the box office phenomenon Twilight, and staff members from the producing studio were asking me to get them in. My credentials allowed me a "plus one" and that was it, not eight other guys.

I walked to the end of the line where the eight other guys were, guided them to the side barriers, and told the security guards, "I'm bringing these gentlemen in."

The security guard said, "No problem," and opened the barriers.

I was able to get this done because I came in a couple hours earlier. Security was comfortable seeing me. When it comes to crunch time, they don't question.

I rarely watch the film when I'm part of a premiere. I have so much adrenaline leading up to the event that I can't sit down with a soda and popcorn to watch a movie.

So, I walked to the barricades on the other side of the street. Usually the general public is kept far away from the red carpet activities. In this case, they were on risers across the street, watching what was going on.

I went to security and said, "I'm going to choose a couple girls, and ask them quietly to come with me. I will be giving them two tickets to the movie premiere."

They nodded and opened a space for me in the barricade.

I approached two young ladies and said, "I'm going to say something to you, but I can't have any reaction. I'm

Putting on a Premiere

These are the two young ladies I picked out of the audience to watch the premiere.

going to give both of you a ticket to the premiere. I need you to not react right now. I'm going to walk you through the barrier. Follow me."

So, I walked the young ladies to where security was waiting for us. I took them to the red carpet so they could have their pictures taken in front of the movie poster, and then I took them to their seats.

I said, "See that gentleman right there?" I pointed to Johnny Brenden. "He's the one you want to thank for your tickets."

Johnny was startled when the ladies ran over to thank him, but he accepted their thanks.

Imagine how I felt to be able to do that for someone else. True fans from the outside looking in were able to see the movie premiere. They felt what it was like to be on the other side of the barrier. That's what dreams are made of.

CHAPTER 24

THE BRENDEN CELEBRITY SUITE

When Johnny Brenden opened the theater in the Palms Casino Resort in Las Vegas, he set aside a large space for his office above the ticket counter, overlooking the lobby of the theater. The space was over 3,000 square feet.

Johnny gave me the responsibility to furnish his office. This was both an honor and a major responsibility because Johnny has impeccable taste.

I asked, "What do you want?"

"Make it an African motif. And do what you need to do."

"I'll take care of it," I assured him.

I began by having his grandfather's desk restored. It was massive with gold leaf inlays on mahogany wood.

When you're shopping for someone else, especially when it's not your money you're spending, it can be quite fun. Better yet, I enjoy negotiating. I would tell Johnny, "This piece runs for $13,000, but I saved $6,000 on it, so we can use that money on this other piece." It felt even better to tell him a piece was worth $20,000, but I got it for only $8,000.

When the office was completed, my associate, Joe Girouard, reached out to the *Wall Street Journal*. They were researching an article on celebrity offices. Joe was able to get Johnny's office featured on the cover of the *Wall Street Journal*. There was a photograph of Johnny sitting on his zebra-skinned ottoman with the office in the background.

After a couple of years, Johnny decided to move some auditoriums around on the property. This was a good time to remodel the office and make it even bigger. It's now around 5,000 square feet.

This time, Johnny commissioned his architect to design an out-of-the-box office space where he could entertain celebrities and VIPs. He wanted a place where celebrities could feel safe and comfortable when they visited his theater for different events.

But after spending thousands on the architect, Johnny threw away the renderings and designed the space himself. He spent several million dollars to get the office suite to look the way he wanted. The first thing you notice when you walk into the Brenden Celebrity Suite is the 22-foot shark tank, which has been featured on *Animal Planet*. The next thing you notice is the b.b. Simon designed Swarovski crystal mirrors. Some of them have televisions behind them. When the television is on, it shines through the mirror.

There are several theater-sized movie screens. The carpet is from Africa; it took 12 months to make. The doors are made of teak wood from Fiji. There is a wall of photos of Johnny's grandfather with celebrities and Presidents,

Cover photo for the Wall Street Journal *article about Top Executive offices.*

The Brenden Celebrity Suite

I had the single largest office suite in the company with a screening room and reception area.

and artifacts from Johnny's travels decorate shelves and other small spaces throughout.

Toward the back, there are a couple of bathrooms complete with saunas and steam rooms. Next to these rooms is a separate suite that has a bed in it. It's large enough for entertaining, or for people needing to get away from the group in the main part of the suite.

It's one of the most spectacular places I've ever seen, and it truly is a place where celebrities feel comfortable.

On many occasions, we not only invited celebrities to enjoy the space away from the paparazzi, but we even held smaller press events there to control the environment. It is good to have a space that is elegant and large enough to be able to entertain, as well as hold events away from the public.

CHAPTER 25

BRENDEN CELEBRITY STAR

We started giving out Brenden Celebrity Stars to celebrities in 2005, some of whom include Robin Leach, Sylvester Stalone, Cuba Gooding Jr., Shaquille O'Neal, Dwayne Johnson, and Kid Rock, just to name a few.

From the time he was a kid, Johnny remembered the excitement that came from the stars and handprints created along Hollywood Boulevard in front of his grandfather's theater.

The first star to be unveiled at Brenden Theatres was for Johnny's grandmother, actress Rhonda Fleming. Johnny surprised her with a dedication during the CineVegas Film Festival. Dennis Hopper, the host of the festival, did the unveiling.

As mentioned, Kid Rock was one of the people we selected for a Celebrity Star. We reached out to his

My Life on the Red Carpet

Me and Shaquille O'Neil at the acceptance of his Brenden celebrity star, at Brenden Theatres at The Palms Casino Resort, Las Vegas.

management, who agreed that he would accept it when he came to Las Vegas to perform at the Pearl inside of the Palms.

My associate, Joe Girouard, was going to handle the details for the presentation after the concert.

When celebrities come into town, they usually have tight schedules, or at least their handlers have tight schedules for them.

Celebrities ultimately do whatever they want. Joe knew how important this presentation was to Johnny Brenden, so he worked with Kid Rock's management to make sure there was time in his schedule for the presentation. Joe made sure he was in the green room when the concert

Me, Joe Girouard, and Shaquille O'Neil

ended, ready to escort Kid Rock to where his star would be unveiled.

As you can imagine, it was a mess in the green room; publicists, handlers, and lots of other people were moving around frantically. Worse, Kid Rock wasn't feeling well. He was off the stage and had disappeared within five minutes without coming over for the presentation of his star. Joe didn't have control over whether Kid Rock was sick or not, but no one likes to deliver bad news.

The long walk to the Brenden Celebrity Suite was even longer for Joe because he knew Johnny would be disappointed.

And he was. It was a major letdown for Johnny.

When I got word of what had happened, I ranted and raved. I should have been there. If I had, I would have made it happen, no offense to Joe. I got on the phone with the vice president of the company to express my frustration. He said, "I know, Jerry. You would have made it happen. It's just that you weren't there. Let's try it next time."

A couple of months later, Kid Rock was performing again at the Pearl. For various reasons, I wasn't able to get to Las Vegas for the performance. So, I purchased the same guitar Kid Rock plays, and shipped it to the Palms Casino Resort for him to sign. We would frame it and put it in the Brenden Celebrity Suite for people to see.

The guitar arrived, and everything was staged. I was determined to make sure everything went as planned this time. I coordinated everything by phone. I made sure people were ready to escort Kid Rock from the green room to his Brenden Celebrity Star in the lobby of the theater.

I was on the phone every couple of minutes, making sure photographers were nearby, and that nothing was in the way between the Pearl and the Celebrity Star.

Finally, Kid Rock was there. They got photos of him with his Brenden Celebrity Star, as well as of him signing the guitar.

Johnny was happy, Joe was excited, and I was able to co-ordinate it all via my cell phone from Northern California.

A couple of weeks later, I was in Las Vegas for a different performance. I was backstage at the Pearl and saw Kid Rock. He was talking to a couple of gentlemen in sweat suits. I walked over and introduced myself.

I said, "Excuse me. I'm Jerry Olivarez, Johnny Brenden's publicist."

"How's Johnny?" he asked.

I assured him that Johnny was doing well, and that we were all thankful that he took the time to sign the guitar and get some photos with his Brenden Celebrity Star. "We really do appreciate it," I concluded.

"No worries," he said. "Anything for my buddy Johnny."

I said, "Thank you very much."

When I turned to leave, he said something to the other two gentlemen, and all three of them laughed. That piqued my interest, so I turned back, and asked, "Excuse me, what did you say?"

"I told these guys that you are a publicist, and you look like a publicist. They are publicists, and they don't look like publicists, even though they probably make more money than you do."

You wouldn't have thought they were publicists by how they were dressed, nor how they handled themselves.

The way you dress makes an impact. How I dress has always helped me out. Even as a young man, I always dressed nice. I would wear dress shirts, carefully pressed, with nice pants, and perfectly combed hair.

I noticed that it makes a difference in how people perceive you.

For instance, I once went to an Oscar De La Hoya fight. I was there about two hours early. As I walked to the gate, the security guard opened the ropes for me without checking my ID.

I asked who was in charge of security. They radioed my request, and a man came to greet me.

"I need three seats for Johnny Brenden."

He turned away from me and radioed to someone to hold the seats. "It's taken care of," he said.

I thanked him and left.

Now remember, I just walked in without credentials. The guards believed I was someone important because of how I was dressed and how I carried myself. And because I commanded an air of authority, I was able to get pricey, restricted seats for my client.

It doesn't cost a lot to look good. I know people who paid $20 for the same item I paid $500 for. You can get a pair of dress pants for $6, the same that I might pay $75 for at a nice department store. A tie for $6 looks almost as good as a tie that I would pay $75 for. Don't let perceived costs stand in the way of looking the part. As Jerry Wientraub says, "Act the part, dress the part, and you will eventually grow into the suit."

CHAPTER 26

VISITING THE MANSION

I got a phone call one day from Johnny. "Jerry, what are you doing?"

"Nothing specific. Just getting things done."

"Okay, this is what I want you to do. I want you to pack, and meet me in Beverly Hills tomorrow. We are going to the Playboy Mansion."

It turned out that George Maloof was having a kick-off party at the mansion for the Palms Casino Resort, and I was a guest.

Of course, this was something a lot of guys have on their bucket lists. When I was a kid, I can remember seeing the logo of the Playboy Bunny on the building of the offices in Los Angeles and wondering about the beautiful women inside.

"Okay, great. I'll be there." I said.

I flew to Burbank that night and got a room at the Four Seasons Hotel in Beverly Hills where Johnny was staying. I wanted to be ready to leave when Johnny was.

It was late the next day when I got a call that the limo was ready. I went downstairs and joined Johnny for the drive to the famous Playboy Mansion.

It was unbelievable, and it was everything everyone has said about it, more than you can imagine. There were tents around the property, and beautiful women strolled across the grounds. Celebrities stood in clumps. As you know, there is a zoo there. And, of course, I visited the famous grotto with its pool and playroom.

Girls were lounging everywhere. Playmates were running into the mansion and out. I was overwhelmed with it all. It was hard to focus. All I have are snapshots of memory from the experience.

As I wandered, I heard someone yelling, "Jerry. Jerry. My brother from another mother. I love you."

I turned to greet Vince Neil. "Hi, Vince. How are you?"

He hugged me like we'd been friends forever, and then he released me and wandered into a nearby group of people.

I turned, and there was Robin Leach. I walked over to him, reintroduced myself, and we struck up a conversation. That's when our friendship truly began.

Shortly after that is when Hugh Hefner walked onto the grounds. Of course, conversation ceased as all heads turned to watch him escort a pair of beautiful ladies into the crowd.

I timed my approach to the bar so that I was there when he arrived. I turned to him and said, "Excuse me Mr.

Visiting the Mansion

Hefner, would it be okay with you if we got a picture of us together?"

He nodded his consent, even though he rarely allows people to take his picture.

A couple of years later, when we were opening the only Playboy Club in the world at the Palms, we presented Hugh Hefner with a Brenden Celebrity Star.

I was in charge of making sure the talent was on time and that everything went smoothly. I went to the Playboy Suite to escort everyone to the ceremony. Hugh came out with the three girls he was dating at the time, and we rode the elevator down together, traversed the casino, and positioned everyone for the press and the ceremony.

Entertainment Tonight, Access Hollywood, TMZ, and all the usual suspects were there to record the ceremony.

After the presentation, we followed Hugh Hefner back to the Playboy penthouse suite in the Fantasy Tower. I had

a camera crew with me; *Extra* and *Entertainment Tonight* also had crews. After they interviewed Mr. Hefner, they had to leave, but I kept my camera crew with me to film behind the scenes. They captured Hugh and me talking. I was able to put that footage into a 20 minute documentary that I show students when I visit colleges.

A couple of weeks after that experience, we did another Brenden Celebrity Star presentation for the reality show *The Girls Next Door*. That is when I found out that Hugh Hefner is a true gentleman.

Holly Madison's mother arrived late. The ceremony was over, and the photographers had left. Hef was headed back to the Playboy Suite.

When I was told about Holly's mother, I approached Hef, "Excuse me. Holly's mother has just shown up. She wants a picture with you and Holly at the star."

Even though he is getting up there in years, he walked back from his penthouse suite to the theater to take photos with Holly and her mother in front of her Celebrity Star. Her mother was even able to pose in a few pictures with her daughter.

CHAPTER 27

THE INFAMOUS O.J. SIMPSON

One evening during the 2005 CineVegas Film Festival, I was standing with Johnny Brenden and some others in Nine Steakhouse waiting for our table.

CineVegas was the baby of Danny and Robin Greenspun, the heads of a highly prominent family with deep roots in Las Vegas. Every year thousands of people, including many celebrities, would flock to the Brenden Theatres at the Palms Casino Resort to watch an impressive line-up of independent movies, as well as a few major ones, like the opening of *Oceans Thirteen*. Unfortunately, the film festival ended after the passing of Dennis Hopper, who was a prominent part of the festival.

During the 2005 CineVegas, such celebrities as Christopher Walken, Nicolas Cage, and Ann-Margret walked the red carpet. The festival closed that year with the world premiere of *Land of the Dead*.

My Life on the Red Carpet

With all that was going on during the festival, we rarely left the property. Dinners, such as the one we were having that evening at Nine Steakhouse, were working dinners.

While we were talking, I noticed a prominent figure to my right, with four or five people around him. He looked

Holding The Oscar of Jon Landau, Avatar producer, at Cinevegas.

at me, and I quickly turned my head and continued talking to my group.

But out of the corner of my eye, I saw him move toward us. He singled me out, even though I was the least important person in the group. Because I was wearing a suit and tending to Johnny, he must have assumed I was someone important.

He stuck out his hand and said, "Hi. I'm O.J. Simpson."

I didn't want to shake his hand, and when I did, an odd feeling coursed through me. "I'm Jerry."

He then went on to tell me that he was filming a documentary.

Trevor Groth Dir. of Programming, Sundance film Festival; me; Mike Plant, Technical Dir. Sundance Film Festival.

I politely introduced him to Johnny Brenden and the others in our group. We exchanged a few words until our table was announced, and I assumed we were done with O.J.

The next day, we were hosting the red carpet event for the world premiere of *Deuce Bigelow*. Things were at their usual frenzy. Limos were lining up in front of the casino. Celebrities and personalities were filing along the red carpet. A crush of cameras recorded the festivities.

It was Johnny Brenden's turn on the red carpet. While Johnny and George were being interviewed, people suddenly start calling out, "O.J. O.J."

We turned, and there was Mr. Simpson, walking onto the red carpet with his documentary crew. The problem was, he wasn't on the guest list. His crew certainly should not have been on the carpet.

We exited quickly, to move out of the way of the distraction.

After the film started, the celebrities retired to the Brenden Celebrity Suite for a reception. And there was O.J., sitting on the desk that was Ted Mann's. Next to him was a crystal machete. It was a gift from Leor, the jeweler from Las Vegas. It was about a foot and a half long with different colors of crystal in it.

Despite all its beauty, it was surreal seeing O.J. holding it. While I was watching, he picked up the huge knife.

After that occurrence, Johnny put stanchions and ropes around the desk, and a sign that says "Do not touch. Do not sit." After all, the desk is priceless, with its gold leaf inlay, not to mention its history.

Even though O.J. wasn't invited, Johnny still thanked him. We all shook hands, and I moved away to attend to the crowd.

A few minutes later, a gentleman approached me saying he was the producer of O.J.'s documentary.

"Nice to meet you," I replied. "I'm Jerry Olivarez, Johnny's publicist."

He said, "I know who you are. O.J. said to make sure I introduced myself to you."

A couple of weeks later, I receive a package in the mail. I opened it to find a letter: "Jerry, I took this picture and thought you might want to have it." The accompanying framed photograph showed O.J. and me.

I felt creeped out looking at that photo. I have a lot of photographs of myself with other celebrities hanging in my office, but that particular one is in a drawer, upside down, so no one will see it.

CHAPTER 28

HONORED BY THE FIRST LADY OF CALIFORNIA, MARIA SHRIVER

One day I was in my office at Brenden Theatres when I received a phone call from the office of the First Lady of the State of California, Maria Shriver. Her team contacted me because they were working on a childhood obesity summit that was going to take place in Sacramento.

The woman on the phone began to tell me about how the First Lady wanted to draw attention to the problem of childhood obesity. She went on to tell me about the problems childhood obesity causes.

I interrupted her, "I'm in. I'm in. What would you like me to do?"

She said, "The First Lady will call you or Johnny Brenden to discuss implementing a healthy choice program in your theaters."

"Absolutely. I understand the problem. Just last year, I was diagnosed with diabetes. I know the significance of the problem. I will do whatever I can for the First Lady to bring more awareness to this issue."

So, we set up a healthy choice campaign at Brenden Theatres, letting people know they could order healthy things, like bottled water and trail mix, at our concession stands. We didn't want to shove anything down the public's throat, but we did want to let them know that they have a choice.

Our efforts were significant to Maria Shriver because she wanted to have a movie theater on board with her campaign. Everyone on her team told her this would never happen because theaters sell junk food. They make money selling popcorn, soft drinks, candy, pretzels, hot dogs, and so on. There was no way a movie theater was going to indulge her requests to offer healthier choices.

But to her team's surprise, Brenden Theatres said yes.

I was invited to Sacramento for the summit where there were people like Dr. Phil, Dr. Oz, and of course Arnold Schwarzenegger, who was then the Governor of California.

I stayed in the same hotel as the first couple the night before the summit. The next day I was in the lobby when Maria Shriver arrived. The black SUVs pulled up as Secret Service poured into the lobby. They also swarmed around Maria as they ushered her through the lobby doors.

Just as she entered the lobby, Maria looked at me and turned as if she were going to come over to me.

I turned away, thinking there was no way she knew who I was. I believed she thought I was someone else, and I didn't want her to be embarrassed.

Honored by the First Lady of California, Maria Shriver

Later that evening, I arrived at the Governor's Mansion for the summit. Maria Shriver was surrounded by a group of people and photographers.

One of her team members came over to me and said she wanted to introduce me to the First Lady.

As I approached the group, Maria turned around and said, "Oh, Jerry." She grabbed me and wrapped her arms around me. Obviously she had seen a picture of me, so she knew who I was at the hotel.

She enthusiastically introduced me to everyone in the circle. "This is Jerry from Brenden Theatres. They are the first movie theater to implement healthier choices at their concession stands." Photographers started taking pictures of me being introduced to the group.

After the introductions, the First Lady excused herself to prepare for her speech. There were over 150 people attending, including the movers-and-shakers in the state of California. What was exciting for me was that Brenden Theatres was the only company Maria mentioned by name in her speech. She said, "One day, I would like to walk into a movie theater like Brenden Theatres and have the ability to make a healthier choice."

People came up to me afterward saying, "Wow Jerry, you're the only one she mentioned out of everyone here." That is how significant this program was to Mrs. Shriver.

Unfortunately, the program didn't take off. When you do something like this, you have to invest a lot of money and time to let the public know about the program. But after a while, if it doesn't take off, it doesn't take off. We did heed Maria Shriver's request, and we were proud to be a part of her program. We only wish the public also supported her initiative. In the end, even with the best intentions, you have to listen to your customers.

This should in no way diminish the First Lady's efforts. She did a lot of good with her campaign, drawing attention to the problem of childhood obesity. I look forward to working with her again in the future.

CHAPTER 29

WHAT LOVE IS, THE MOVIE

For the premiere of *What Love Is*, I went to the Henderson Executive Airport to pick up Cuba Gooding, Jr. He was joined by his friend, Matthew Lillard, who played Shaggy in the live-action movie *Scooby Do*.

I had the limo meet them on the tarmac and drive us back to Brenden Theatres at the Palms. As we drove, I took a couple phone calls.

When I finished, Cuba asked, "Are you Johnny's publicist?"

"Yes, I am."

"Will you do me a favor? My name is pronounced Cuba with a hard Q. I want to make sure you get it right because if you don't get it right, people are going to repeat what you say."

I said, "I appreciate that, and I will keep it in mind."

At the Palms, I accompanied Cuba and Matt through the check-in process and showed them to their room. We then arranged to have dinner later at Nova Italiano in the Fantasy Tower.

We had a very nice dinner, laughing and talking. We had a photographer with us, so before we left the restaurant, I asked Cuba if we could get a picture together before he headed into the crowd.

He agreed. We stood for the photographer, and Cuba grabbed my head and started kissing me on the forehead. The photographer kept clicking as I busted up laughing. I never expected anything like that.

Later, after the premiere and after-party, we wandered out to the pool.

"Jerry," Matt Lillard asked, "I have this tuxedo shirt, but I don't have the cufflinks or buttons. Can you find some for me?"

I immediately began looking. The Palms didn't have any, so I drove to the mall, where I found what he needed.

Matt reimbursed me for the cufflinks and buttons, of course. But, more important, he was overwhelmed that I had not only found them for him, but took the time to get them myself. He said, "Jerry, anything you want, whatever, let me know. If you need me to show up at a birthday party or whatever, I will."

After about a year, I did need a favor. I picked up the phone, and called Matt. Someone wanted him in a movie, and I had a direct connection. He took my call and agreed to read the script.

After reading it, however, he graciously declined the role. But that's not the point. Because I had taken the extra time and applied the extra effort when he needed me, he didn't feel put out when I sent him the script. Most people would have simply sent him a script or asked him a favor after meeting him. But because I gave first, he didn't feel put-upon. He also felt comfortable enough to tell me why it wasn't a project for him.

While doing unexpected things for people does give you access to them, don't believe for a moment they are obligated to you. All you've gained is the opportunity to call upon them later. Expecting a return for your favors only causes resentment. The best reward for going the extra mile is appreciation. Accept it, and be thankful for anything else that comes your way.

CHAPTER 30

DEVASTATING NEWS

Delivering bad news is difficult, and no one likes doing it. But the more responsibility you have, the more bad news you'll have to give.

Is there any worse news than that your mother has died?

At 7:00 in the morning, my phone rang. The ID said it was Johnny Brenden's sister. It can't be good news that early in the morning.

"Hello, Blythe."

"Mom just died," she cried into the phone. "I can't get a hold of Johnny."

I said, "Blythe, I am sorry for your loss. I will take care of it."

"No," she said, "Someone needs to be there with him."

"Don't worry. I will take care of everything and get back in contact with you."

That's a tough way to wake up. While Johnny's mother had been diagnosed with Parkinson's disease, nobody expected her to pass so quickly.

I immediately got into work mode. I was in Concord, CA, and Johnny was in Las Vegas. I called George Maloof, the owner of the Palms. It wasn't my usual hour for calling him, and I'm sure I woke him up.

When he answered I said, "George, could you please do me a favor? Johnny's mother has unexpectedly passed. He's home right now, asleep, and I need someone to go to his penthouse and give him the news. This isn't something he should hear over the phone."

George said he was on his way.

I chose George Maloof because it's better to receive news of that kind from a close, personal friend.

Next, I called Johnny's girlfriend at the time. She lived in Huntington Beach, California. When she answered, I asked what she was doing right then.

"I am having breakfast with my children."

"You need to get to Las Vegas as soon as possible. Johnny lost his mother this morning. You need to be with him."

I then suggested that she pack to go to the funeral with him in Minnesota.

She said she'd look for a flight immediately.

I called George back. He answered without saying hello. "Jerry, I haven't left yet. I'm waiting for a car to pick me up. I will let you know when I get there."

"I'm calling security at his building to make sure you have clearance to go straight up to his penthouse," I said.

After that call, I called Blythe to let her know that everything was in the works. I reassured her that Johnny was sound asleep. He wouldn't hear the news until George arrived.

Then, I began making my own travel plans. Johnny's girlfriend called to give me her flight number.

Within the hour, George called back, "Jerry, Johnny is here, and he wants to be left alone."

"That's fine, George. His girlfriend will be there in a couple hours."

Now that I knew Johnny was okay, I called the executive vice president and CFO of the company to let them know what happened.

It wasn't until three hours later that I first spoke with Johnny. I expressed my sadness for his loss and assured him that I would take care of everything. "You know I'm flying to Minnesota to be there for you."

"Thanks, Jerry."

At the funeral, I realized that it doesn't matter how much money you have, how many mansions you have, or what toys you have. We all end up in a hole in the ground with a mound of soil on top of us.

When you get caught up in the day-to-day accumulation of wealth, don't lose the understanding that we are only borrowing life for a period of time.

Johnny had me as his confidant. He could have hired anyone for my position, but you cannot buy loyalty. He never had to worry, nor did his sister consider, whether or not I would come through in a crisis. Blythe knew I would do my best to lessen the blow for Johnny. She also knew she had put the task in the best hands possible. She didn't need to tell me what to do, nor did she have to worry about whether or not I was on the clock. She knew I would handle the situation with the best tact. Why did she have this confidence in me? Because I had proven myself long before the crisis occurred.

CHAPTER 31

SUCCESS IS ABOUT SHOWING UP

You may not remember the movie *Stripperella*, starring Pamela Anderson. It was based on a comic book character created by Stan Lee.

Over time, interest in the movie went away, and POW! Entertainment wanted to revive the character.

Some years ago, Marvel Comics was sold to Disney and they retained the right to have a first look at anything Stan and his company, POW! Entertainment, create.

The revitalization idea involved severing any ties with Pam Anderson to avoid problems, so they redesigned the character to have red hair and an overall different look.

My associate, Joe Girouard, and I worked out an agreement with POW! to represent the Stripperella franchise, which we then took to the Palms Casino Resort. We thought a Stripperella themed penthouse suite at the Palms would be a great association.

I wanted to bring the idea to George Maloof personally. So, I flew to Las Vegas and looked for George. I knew he is rarely in his office; he usually walks the casino floor, watching over things.

When he saw me looking for him, he came over to give me a hug. "Jerry, walk with me, and don't leave my side. There's someone over there I don't want to talk to."

"No worries, George."

As we walked, I outlined my idea for the themed suite. I told him the folks at POW! Entertainment estimated the franchise deal to be in the multi-millions. Then I asked, "Are you interested in this project?"

"Fuck yeah."

"Okay, great. Now we're talking about merchandising, clothes, everything. Who do you want me to deal with?"

He pointed to himself, and said, "Me. I want you to deal directly through me. Don't work through my executives. Work through me. Talk to me. I'm going to handle this myself."

That's saying a lot for a man of his prominence. He has a whole team to look over projects, and yet he wanted to oversee things personally. What better opportunity could you have? This was the opportunity of a lifetime.

"When do we start?" he asked.

"Let me talk with Stan Lee and Gill Champion. I will get back to you."

A few weeks later, I set up a conference call with Gil Champion, George Maloof, and myself.

The point of the call was to meet and greet the interested parties. Once everyone had an opportunity to share their vision for the project we would convene later for a face-to-face meeting.

I took the lead on the call because I knew George didn't have a lot of time. He was being driven to another meeting as we spoke.

I started off by having Gill explain his vision for Striperella. Then George shared his thoughts, and I ended the call by thanking everyone for their time and contribution. George concluded with, "Jerry has told me about the project. I'm on board. You have my full support."

We set up a meeting to work out the details.

Two weeks later, I flew back to Las Vegas for the meeting. At the last minute, the assistant to the business partner at POW! called to say that he was unable to attend the meeting and asked if we could please reschedule.

I contacted George Maloof to let him know that we needed to reschedule, and that I would get back to him.

Weeks passed before we were able to reschedule. In the interim, things had changed with Mr. Maloof and the Palms, and the opportunity was no longer there.

You have to strike when the fire is hot. To get a meeting with George Maloof is a very big deal. Canceling that meeting eventually killed the project. In business, do not let important items slip by. When it's time, make the deal.

CHAPTER 32

ROCKY BALBOA AND THE COMPROMISE

The world premiere of *Rocky 5* was at Brenden Theatres in the Palms Casino Resort in Las Vegas. Of course, Sylvester Stallone was slated to be on the red carpet that evening.

He arrived in a stretch black SUV with all the windows blacked out. The vehicle idled for a bit before a sizable group of security guards surrounded the SUV.

His publicist stepped out of the SUV first. We shook hands. I said, "Please introduce me to the head of security."

When she did, I discussed how we were going to move the talent from the vehicle to the red carpet, who would pose and how, and all the other details that have to be worked out.

Finally, it was time. A door opened at the back of the limo, and the security folks gathered in more closely. After a pause, Mr. Stallone emerged behind the cluster of bodies. Together, they moved toward the red carpet, peeling off until only Stallone was left to walk the final steps to the carpet.

The cameras flashed for several minutes before Dennis Hopper walked forward to greet Mr. Stallone. More flashes as they warmly shook hands and turned for the cameras as they struck up a casual conversation.

When the initial frenzy quieted a bit, I approached Mr. Hopper and asked, "Mr. Hopper, would you please introduce Johnny to Mr. Stallone?"

Dennis Hopper smiled and turned to Johnny, motioning him over while I retreated out of camera range. With his arm over Johnny's shoulder, Mr. Hopper made the introduction in front of the cameras.

Why didn't I simply have Johnny introduce himself to Mr. Stallone? After all, it was Johnny's theater, and Mr. Stallone was certainly aware of Johnny's grandfather's place in Hollywood's history.

You see, it is always better to have a friend introduce you to someone else. In this case, Johnny and Dennis Hopper were friends, and Mr. Hopper and Sylvester Stallone were friends. Mr. Hopper was the perfect person to make the introduction.

Each of us has a natural resistance to meeting someone new. This is especially true for celebrities who are inundated with introductions, requests for signing autographs, and groupies trying to get close. When a friend introduces a friend, the ice has been broken, the resistance eased, and there is an opportunity for quick rapport between the two people.

After the introductions were made, and the photo-op concluded, the group moved into the theater. Following his introduction of the movie, Sylvester Stallone walked out of the theater. He sat down to sign the posters and other memorabilia that had been pre-arranged for the event. When the busywork was completed, Mr. Stallone turned to Johnny and invited him to dinner.

You see, celebrities usually leave during the screenings of their movies. They have work to do, like signing posters and memorabilia, and then they usually go to dinner. With their entourage, the party can often be over 12 people.

At the dinner, Johnny and Sylvester made a connection, talking about Ted Mann and Mann's Chinese Theatre in Hollywood. The conversation gave Johnny an in with Stallone.

Johnny also felt more comfortable with the arrangement. Despite being a celebrity in his own right, Johnny is shy.

Once everyone was comfortable, things could flow naturally. I even had the opportunity to talk to Mr. Stallone's people. I struck up a conversation with Jack Gilardi, Mr. Stallone's manager, and Executive VP at ICM Talent Agency. We stayed in contact and became good friends.

Now I get right through when I call ICM. He'll take my call no matter where in the world he is.

When the last Rocky movie was coming out, I called Jack and said, "Jack, we should premiere *Rocky Balboa* at Brenden Theatres."

In a firm tone, Jack replied, "No, Jerry, it can't happen. Sly is connected to the Planet Hollywood."

"Ok, Jack. I'll get back to you."

Johnny wanted the premiere at his theater. It was my job to make it happen. I made a few phone calls and we ended up compromising. The premiere was held at Brenden Theatres, while the after party commenced at the Planet Hollywood. This was a big deal because we had to move everyone from one venue to the other. It can be a logistical nightmare moving that many celebrities and executives between casinos and this was a huge accomplishment. We were dealing with two separate major casinos with different owners. It ended up being a win-win for everyone.

Johnny didn't have me around for what I could not do, rather, for things I could do. As the Executive VP of Brenden Theatres continued to remind me, "If it were easy, someone else would be doing it. That's why we have you." It's all about the execution.

CHAPTER 33

GETTING AN AISLE SEAT

As a second-generation florist, I knew that I would be a florist. Because I knew nothing different, that's what I visualized. Then my career expanded; I became an executive with Brenden Theatres as Johnny Brenden's publicist.

I was flying back to Oakland from Las Vegas on Southwest Airlines. By the time I got around to checking into my flight, my boarding pass number was B43. As you know, the chances of getting an aisle seat with that number are almost nil.

When I boarded, most of the seats were taken; evidently many people were staying on the plane from the previous leg. Worse, the flight attendant told me that every seat would be taken.

I kept moving toward the back, sizing people up. About five rows from the back, I found a row with a large man against the window, and a slim young man in the aisle.

"Excuse me. Do you mind if I sit here?" I asked the young man.

He stood up and said, "Here boss, how 'bout you take this seat?" He moved into the middle, giving me the aisle seat.

I was blown away that someone would give me an aisle seat. "That is very gracious of you."

He said, "That's okay."

As we started to taxi, he turned to me, "Wow, we are leaving Las Vegas on a Friday. You'd think everyone would be flying into Las Vegas on a Friday."

I said, "Yeah, I was here for a meeting."

He said, "I also flew in last night for a meeting." Then he began to tell me about his company. He laid it all out, telling me about how he was handling the accounting and marketing. He also shared with me the situations that he didn't know how to handle.

We talked from the moment we took off to the moment we landed. Now, I don't usually talk when I fly; it's my chance to relax.

When we landed, we exchanged business cards. As I grabbed my bag out of the overhead bin, I thanked him once again for giving me the aisle seat.

"That's okay," he said. "I knew when I saw you that I'd learn something, and I did."

He was smart enough to seek the advice of someone who appeared to be successful. Never be afraid to ask questions.

We only know what we know. It's good to learn from others, to get different perspectives.

CHAPTER 34

MEETING THE KING OF POP

Being a fan of Michael Jackson, and recognizing his contribution to American music, Johnny wanted to present him with a Brenden Celebrity Star.

So, I contacted Joe Jackson and began discussing the possibility of arranging the Celebrity Star for his son, Michael. Mr. Jackson agreed that the Celebrity Star was a good idea; he just needed to work out some details.

When months had passed, I contacted Joe Jackson again. He said, "Look, I'm working on it. Give me some time."

And more time would pass. I'd contact Joe again, only to hear that he was still interested, but needed more time.

This went on for close to two years.

Then I received a phone call. "Hello, this is the head of security for Michael Jackson. I have Michael and Joe Jackson on the phone. Will you take the call?"

The call didn't come as a surprise, although it was a big deal. It was one of those times when you didn't realize you were expecting the call, but when it came, you said, "Oh, this is the call."

Of course, I accepted the call.

When we were connected, I said, "Hello, Mr. Michael Jackson."

A faint voice replied, "Hi."

"Hello, Mr. Joe Jackson."

"Hi."

"How may I help you?"

Joe replied, "Michael has some questions about Brenden Theatres for you."

"Yes?"

Michael proceeded to ask me a series of questions, such as whether or not the theaters were public. Was it a public company? Who owned it? Where were they located? And so on.

I assured him that Johnny Brenden was the sole owner of the theaters. I shared with him who Johnny's grandfather was. I also assured Michael that Johnny and his company were very liquid.

About 15 to 20 minutes into the conversation I said, "You know, Mr. Jackson, if you'd like to talk with Johnny, I'll get him on the phone. He's out of the country right now, but I'm sure I can get a hold of him.

"Oh really?"

"If you don't mind holding for a moment, I'll reach him."

"That would be great."

I put them on hold and called Johnny in the Bahamas. "I have Michael Jackson on the phone. Will you take the call?"

Johnny thought I was joking, and I think he still didn't believe me when I connected him. "Johnny, I have Mr. Michael Jackson on the line. And Mr. Joe Jackson."

They greeted each other and began a brief conversation.

Michael wrapped up the phone call by inviting us to his Las Vegas house to discuss the Brenden Celebrity Star.

In total, the phone conversation lasted 27 minutes and 9 seconds.

I spent the next three months trying to arrange that meeting with Michael Jackson at his house. We would have an appointment, and then a week or a few days before, the meeting would be cancelled because Michael was out of the country, or had to leave unexpectedly. A couple of times they cancelled the day before, after I had already flown to Las Vegas for the appointment.

Finally, his security called to assure me that Michael would be at his house on a certain date and time.

I got on the plane without expectation that this time the meeting would happen. I arrived the day before and drove by the mansion Michael was renting to get a lay of the land.

Satisfied, I retired for the night to be prepared for the next day's meeting.

Johnny drove his Bentley to the meeting. We were stopped by six security guards standing in the middle of the road. They were expecting us, but they wanted us to park to the side of the property and take the side entrance into the house.

When we entered, the children and several bodyguards were in the living room with Joe and Michael. Everyone was quickly ushered out.

Michael was seated on the couch with his back to us, but when everyone was gone, he stood to greet us. Then he took a seat next to his father, and motioned to the two facing couches for Johnny and I to sit.

Since it was summer, the thing that really stood out about the living room was the Christmas tree.

We got to business quickly, but after a few minutes, Michael turned to his father and said something under his breath. Joe looked at me, and then at Johnny, and then nodded yes.

A couple minutes later, Michael again turned to Joe and said something under his breath. Joe nodded again, glancing at me.

After the third time, Johnny interrupted, "Michael, what are you saying?"

Michael laughed and said, "I was just telling Joseph that Jerry looks like Frank DiLeo. Frank is my old manager, and he left me to pursue his acting career and to do the film *Goodfellas*. Jerry reminds me of him.

We laughed, but I didn't know who Frank was. Later, I found pictures of him, and we do have similar facial features.

Soon after our meeting, it was announced that Michael was bringing DiLeo back as his manager, and I like to think that my presence reminded Michael of the good times he had with him. I don't know if it's true or not, but I'd like to think I had something to do with Michael's decision.

Before we left, Michael said he wanted to discuss doing a big project with Johnny. He said, "I want to do the Celebrity Star, but I want to do it around something big. I have an idea, but I can't tell you right now. You have to sign a confidentiality agreement, and then I'll let you know."

"Of course," Johnny said.

"And another thing," Michael started. It turned out that the reason he wanted to know so much about the theater was that he wanted to be able to go to the movies with his children. Someone as famous as he was couldn't enjoy something as simple as sitting in a crowded theater and watching movies.

Johnny agreed to shut down the theaters when Michael wanted a private screening. Sometimes, we would sneak Michael and his children into the theater after a movie had started, so they could experience it like everyone else.

We would stage it so that security and employees of the theater would sit in the back. Then, as the lights came down, Michael and his kids would sneak quickly in, and sit among the security in the back. There was only one time that anyone noticed that it was Michael who was coming in late and taking a seat among all the people in the back of the theater.

At the very end of our visit with Michael and Joe Jackson, Michael mentioned that he had visited the doctor that morning, and that the doctor told him he had walking pneumonia. I specifically remember him saying, "It's true, Joseph, I'm really not feeling well."

The next morning, on *CNN*, it was reported that Michael Jackson was in the hospital with pneumonia. Well, I knew that Michael wasn't in the hospital because we had been in his living room. This shows how the press often changes a story to make it more sensational.

When Johnny and I left Michael Jackson's house, we sat silently in Johnny's Bentley. Finally, I turned to him and said, "Wow, that was history in the making. Michael was talking to just us. No one else was around."

Johnny nodded as he turned the ignition.

It turned out that the big project Michael wanted to launch at his Brenden Celebrity Star unveiling was to be based around his concert tour *This Is It*, which unfortunately never happened.

I remember sitting with Johnny in his office when we heard the news that Michael was being rushed to the hospital. I thought it was just another sensational story.

Within a couple of hours, we heard that Michael was dead. Johnny turned to me and said, "I really wanted to give him the Celebrity Star."

"Don't worry about it," I replied. "We will, only now it will be in his memory."

CHAPTER 35

MICHAEL'S CELEBRITY STAR

We did not present Michael Jackson's posthumous Brenden Celebrity Star during the release of the movie *This Is It*. Instead, we presented it on the one-year anniversary of his death.

Of course there were other commemorative events competing with our unveiling, but it seemed the appropriate time and place to honor Michael.

When I first contacted Joe Jackson to see if he would accept the Brenden Celebrity Star on Michael's behalf, I was told there was a special event in London that Joe would be attending. So I reached out to Frank DiLeo to see if he'd accept the Brenden Celebrity Star on Michael's behalf, and he accepted.

Later, I was told that Jackson would not be going to London after all. I called him and asked if he'd be available to accept the star.

"Of course I will. He was my son."

I mentioned that I had already asked Frank DiLeo to accept the Brenden Celebrity Star.

Joe said, "I don't want to be a part of anything with Frank DiLeo. I don't care for him."

Immediately, I said, "Okay, not a problem. You will accept the star by yourself."

Then, I had to go back to Frank DiLeo. "I'm sorry, plans have changed. Joe Jackson will not be in London after all. He will accept the Brenden Celebrity Star on Michael's behalf."

He said, "I don't mind accepting with Joe."

I replied, "I appreciate that, but we'll just have Joe do it."

In business, it's important to work with personalities and priorities. In this case, Joe Jackson was the most important person to accept the Brenden Celebrity Star. While I did ask Mr. DiLeo, I needed him to step aside to let Joe Jackson have the spotlight.

Some might argue that I should have kept Frank DiLeo, but this is business. Brenden Theatres was better served by having Joe Jackson accept the star. More people know Joe Jackson than Frank DiLeo. With all the press covering different events commemorating Michael Jackson's death, it was important that we get noticed, and Joe's presence helped.

Also, it wasn't my business why Joe didn't want to be there with Frank, but it was my business to make sure Joe was comfortable.

It also wasn't my place to tell Frank why I wouldn't be using him in the ceremony. It was enough to say that Joe

Jackson would be accepting the star without explaining it further. Frank was a true gentleman, and bowed out graciously.

You will often have to go back to someone and tell them that things have changed as you work to create what is best for your company. It's important that you finesse such deals so that no one's ego is hurt in the process. At the end of the day, while it is about business, people's feelings are still involved and you never want to burn a bridge.

MY LIFE ON THE RED CARPET

CHAPTER 36

INVITATION TO SACRAMENTO STATE

Ryan Smith, whom I mentor, asked me to speak for a public relations class he was taking at Sacramento State University. I was honored by the opportunity, and of course agreed.

I tried to think of a way to differentiate myself from others who spoke to the class. I put a production team together and we created a 20-minute video that showed different red carpet events, interviews, and so on. This gave the students a visual representation of what I did, instead of the standard lecture.

I wanted to set the mood so that the students would be excited and my presentation would be well received. So, before the class started, I set out bottles of water, movie theater candy, and bags of popcorn on a table outside the classroom. As the students came in, they grabbed whatever they wanted and prepared for a movie experience.

As they found their seats, a slide show ran different photos of me with different celebrities and Johnny Brenden. The song, *Viva Las Vegas*, accompanied the slide show. Then, once I was introduced, they showed the video.

After that, I spoke to the students about my life experiences and what I've learned along the way. For me, it was an honor to share with them, but I don't think I'm that special of a person. I've had great opportunities and some

Dr. Timothy Howard and I with his signed copy of my book in his office at Sacramento State University.

amazing experiences, but the students can achieve so much more in life.

After my conversation with them, they lined up to get pictures with me and shake my hand. They asked me if I had a book. I didn't, of course, but the students wanted to learn more from my experiences. The response was so great that I was asked to come back the following year to speak.

The next year, I provided a similar experience for the students, with similar results. The students lined up, took pictures with me, and asked me if I had a book. I looked at them, and saw in their eyes that they were inspired and that they wanted to be further inspired.

After the class, I had dinner with Professor Howard, the professor of the class, and the advisor of the chapter of the Public Relations Student Society of America that Ryan started at the university. He said, "Jerry, when you come and speak to my students, for the next three weeks or so, there is a dynamic about them. They are enthusiastic. They are excited. I really appreciate it when you speak to them."

This immediately made me think about the students and their constant requests for a book. I now felt a responsibility to write one, as long as it allowed me to inspire, enlighten, and give some sort of insight into this industry.

"You know what, I'm going to write a book," I declared. "I'm going to do it." It was more out of feeling an obligation than a need to tell my story. If these students were excited, if they were inspired by my stories, then I owed it to them to write a book that would give them more than a 50 minute experience with me.

My Life on the Red Carpet

Dear Mr. Jerry Olivarez,

I am writing in regards to our trip to Las Vegas. During our trip to the dessert you displayed a human trait that is not very common. It isn't something you can learn or teach; it's something that is embedded in one from the time of early childhood. It is something to be truly proud of, and I would like to say I am honored to be a part of something so beautiful.

This past weekend was priceless for my future, and it was spent with someone with whom I would not have traded for all the gold in the world. You continue to inspire, and educate even in the face of adversity. The meetings you took me to should have been locked and closed door, yet you had the faith in me to be able to represent you and for that, I am truly thankful and honored.

You define what is great about humanity, and it still amazes me to this day. I do not know one other person who bends over like you do to show and share the lifestyle you have. You are humble and deserving of all of your success. Others in your position seem to be eager to exclude when you go out of your way to include.

I sat back and watched you operate a few times this past weekend and I truly got a big smile on the inside because of the way you carry yourself. You are professional and powerful, yet you are respectful of even the smallest individual in your company. Your loyalty to my future success is THE driving force behind my success to date.

From the kid who liked a watch to the kid who got to sit in a board meeting at the Palms. Who would have thought, and who would have believed them.

To be a humanitarian is to show the utmost humility and desire to give to others what is great about human nature. To be a philanthropist is to offer ones self for the betterment of another. (All definitions are my opinion.) You are invested in the charity of the Smith family and we will be forever grateful to you for it.

I hope reading this gives you goose bumps for writing it has caused them to appear all over my body. You are great, and probably the most inspiring person I have ever met.

Do not ever change, and believe me I will return the favor one day my friend. Be proud, you did your job with me; I have grown up, something without you I would not have been able to achieve at this point in my life.

Love you my man.

Ryan was the catalyst for this experience and the realization that I should write a book to inspire others.

Later, I told him, "You know what? For your graduation, I'm going to fly you out to Las Vegas. You will shadow me for three days, and it will be around a world premiere so that you can get a real insight of what it is like to execute all of this."

Well, he graduated that year, and I flew him out to Las Vegas. At the time, I normally stayed at the Bellagio in one of the beautiful center penthouse suites overlooking the famous fountains. They have two bedrooms and 2,000 square feet of space.

For three days, Ryan shadowed me through boardroom meetings with George Maloof and the top executives of the Palms Casino Resort, as well as the people from Sony Studios. He was able to experience all the ins and outs behind the scenes at premiers, along with the logistics that need to be considered to pull off a media event. And, of course, he got to attend the premiere.

I knew he was inspired, but I didn't realize how much until three days after he got back home. He sent me the nicest thank-you note that I have received in my life. It took me several times to read it before I could read it without getting choked up. In fact, today, I still can't read it without getting emotional.

I was so filled with gratitude that I was able to affect another human being like that. It reminded me how important it is to have mentors in life, to have others share with you their experiences and knowledge.

I look back to when I was the age of 13. I had mentors all around me. For instance, the gentleman I worked for at the gas station, and the people running the recreation center that I worked at after school. These people were mentors. I knew I could pick up the phone at any time and ask them questions, knowing full well that their answers would always have my best interests at heart.

As I grew up, my mother and father were the greatest mentors. I went to them for advice. I'd ask their opinion, knowing they had my best interests in mind and heart. They wouldn't make decisions for me. When I'd gathered all the information I could, I would ultimately make my own decisions based on their advice. It is important to take ownership of what you do and the decisions you make.

I've had several mentors throughout my life. Remember how important Greg Warner was to my first flower shop? I probably would have never opened a shop without his guidance and mentorship. And even if I had, I'm sure I would have struggled without the knowledge he shared with me.

Johnny Brenden was another important mentor in my life. After all, he is the one who introduced me to the world of entertainment.

It wasn't until I became other peoples' mentors that I understood the rewards that my mentors received from working with me. Arguably, I get more satisfaction from being a mentor than those I mentor. It is a very special feeling to help another human being with no hidden agenda, and with the expectation of receiving nothing in return.

If you are so lucky and blessed to have a mentor in your life, thank them. If you don't have a mentor, find one. They will help you make decisions in your life, and provide guidance as you move forward.

CHAPTER 37

THIS IS IT

My encounter with Don King happened during the Brenden Celebrity Star unveiling for the Jackson family at the premiere of *This Is It*.

Months before this unveiling, Joe Jackson had accepted Michael Jackson's Brenden Celebrity Star on his behalf. Now he was back at the premiere of Michael's final movie, accepting a Celebrity Star for himself and his family.

We worked it out with Sony to do a special screening of the movie. It was to be released at midnight Friday morning, but we were able to show it at 7:00 PM on Thursday.

It was the biggest media event the Palms Casino Resort had ever had. All the networks were there, press from around the world, and many major celebrity television shows sent their best reporters. So I was stressed and focused, making sure everything went smoothly, and that no one would be aware of all the work that went into the event.

In the midst of all of this, I was passed a note that Don King wanted to talk with me.

With an event this large, I had been getting a lot of requests from people wanting to attend the Celebrity Star unveiling. The problem was, we had only about 20 seats for VIPs. And at that point the list was over 60, plus we needed space for the media, and an area for on-lookers.

I called Don King's number. When I told him who I was, he announced, "I was invited by Joe Jackson. I'll be coming."

"That's great, Mr. King. We'll have two seats for you in the VIP."

"No. That's not enough. I need more."

You know what a big personality Don King is. The last thing I needed during this overwhelming event was his displeasure and demands. "How many do you need, Mr. King?"

"I will have ten people with me."

"I can't do that."

"What do you mean you can't do that?"

"I can give you two VIP seats."

"But I'm Don King."

"Sir, I simply don't have enough room."

"But Joe Jackson invited me. He knows I'm coming."

Thinking quickly, I came up with, "I'll have two seats. The other people can stand nearby."

After a pause, he said, "Okay, I'll show up in a little while."

Don King and I in the Brenden Celebrity Suite after the Jackson family's Brenden Celebrity Star unveiling

After the screening and unveiling of the Brenden Celebrity Star, I moved the press and VIPs to the Brenden Celebrity Suite.

There were probably 150 people in the suite. Normally, we don't have that many people assembled when interviews are happening, but it was the only space in the casino where we had a controlled environment. I organized everyone so that each media outlet could interview Joe Jackson.

Joe Jackson was being interviewed by *Access Hollywood* and *Entertainment Tonight* when, suddenly, the huge voice of Don King boomed throughout the facility. He was waving his flags and causing a general distraction.

The louder he got, the louder everyone else began to speak to be heard over his voice.

I called Ryan over and requested that he ask Don King to be quiet. Ryan is about six foot three, much taller than me, and more formidable. But he said, "Please don't ask me to do that." After all, Don King was once convicted (albeit pardoned) of killing a man with his bare hands.

I looked at Ryan and said, "You just need to go to Don King, and tell him he needs to be quiet."

"Please don't ask me to do that."

"I need you to do it."

Reluctantly he approached Don King. He said, "Jerry Olivarez asked me to come over and ask you to please keep your voice down."

Sure enough, Don King did quiet down.

But it still wasn't enough. A couple of times, I had to raise my voice to tell people to keep their voices down. I felt like I was yelling, "Ladies and gentleman, please be quiet. We are filming right now. If you don't, we will have to escort you out."

I wasn't afraid to have security throw out Don King, if it had come to that, because Joe Jackson was the one being honored, and in light of his son Michael's recent death, nothing else that evening was more important.

Of course, I didn't want the press talking about Michael Jackson's death to his father. I told them that they could only talk about the legacy Michael left the world.

A very popular network morning show tried to slide in a question about Michael's doctor. I stopped the interviewer. I said, "We talked about this earlier. We are going to keep things positive."

The reporter didn't stop with the question about the controversy of Michael's death, so I stopped the interview.

The cameras turned to me while Joe removed his microphone. I said to the camera, "I told you, this will not work."

Even though I was firm with the reporter that night, he and I have had several opportunities to talk on the phone and in person. He wasn't accustomed to his interviews being cut short like that, but I shut him down in such a way that he felt comfortable reaching out to me later.

Be careful of your responses, because you never know when you will see people again.

Unfortunately, the next day they reported that Joe Jackson shut down the interview himself once questions turned to the subject of Michael's children. The truth is that I shut the interview down, not Joe Jackson.

After the interviews were over, Don King came over to me. I don't mind saying that I was a little intimidated. He said, "Jerry, I'm going to have a press conference tomorrow. You should come over. I will be talking about you."

I didn't attend the press conference; it was taking place on another casino's property. He was promoting a fight. And no, he didn't mention me.

The point is you need to control the environment while being respectful to everyone, even those who are making your job difficult. Truth be told, I was not only intimated, but I was grateful that he attended my event. After all, he is the great Don King.

With James Gandolfini at the private Foundation Room at the top of Mandalay Bay, Las Vegas after the premier of the Michael Jackson's Cirque du Sole show, One

My Life on the Red Carpet

CHAPTER 38

TWO FOR THE MONEY

When the movie *Two for the Money* came out, we held a celebrity screening at the Brenden Theatres in the Palms. Celebrity screenings are different from world premieres. If the studio titles something a world premiere, they are sometimes contractually obligated to fly out the talent, put them up, feed them, and so on. But with celebrity screenings, they bypass this obligation.

There are a lot of celebrity screenings in Las Vegas, because the talent is either already there, or they don't mind visiting. Jeremy Piven is one of the latter celebrities.

When we announced that we were having a celebrity screening of his movie, Jeremy Piven let us know that he would attend along with his friend DJ Common. At the time, I didn't know who DJ Common was.

It was one of the most stressful premieres I've done, partly because of the tight budget I had from Brenden

Theatres. I was able to book Jeremy and DJ Common for $99 each on a Southwest flight out of Burbank. I have found, over the years, that celebrities aren't as demanding as their handlers and publicists, so I wasn't worried about the rather ordinary flight I had booked the celebrities on.

I was having dinner at Little Buddha at the Palms when I received a phone call from someone connected to Jeremy Piven. I told him the flights were taken care of, and gave him all the necessary information about the flights and accommodations.

He said, "You don't have a charter?"

"No, I don't. I'm not going to charter a flight from Burbank to Las Vegas. That is a 45-minute flight."

"Jeremy can't fly Southwest."

I said, "I fly Southwest."

He said, "Jerry, it can't happen. It will be embarrassing to tell him that he is flying Southwest."

"Fine," I sighed. "What do you need?"

"We need first-class for Jeremy and DJ Common."

I was reluctant because I didn't want to go back to the well and ask for more money; I have too much integrity for that. When I'm given a budget, I stay within it. I don't want to be questioned. I don't want anyone asking "This is your budget, but what is it really going to cost us?"

I checked, and first-class tickets for two came to $1,500. I took the money right out of my pocket, because staying within budget was worth more to me than the money.

I called the handler back and told him the new flight numbers and times. "Who's going to pick them up?" he asked.

"I'm sending a car for them."

"Jerry, you've got to be there to pick them up personally. This is Jeremy and DJ Common."

The problem was I had to coordinate the event. I couldn't leave the property to pick them up at the airport. That would take me of the property for over an hour.

But I realize that I represent my client, in this case Brenden Theatres, so I took a Palms limo to the airport. I greeted the men as they came down the escalator to the baggage claim area in the McCarran airport. We got their bags and headed back to the Palms. The whole time, I was beyond frustrated; I was approaching anger.

I always say to never let them see you sweat. For all the hassles, no one knew what was going on behind the scenes, the difficulties I was having, nor the struggles it took to pull off the event with a trip to the airport in the middle of preparations.

As we pulled up to the casino, I recognized Jeremy's excitement when he saw the Palms marquee. There was his name, written larger than he'd ever seen it before.

In the end, everything went well, even for all the stress leading up to the event.

One of the more important things Johnny Brenden instilled in me was follow-through. If you make a promise, keep it, and always be humble.

Follow-through is what will differentiate you from a lot of people. If you are going to show up, or not show up, call ahead. Let them know. Little things like that can be monumental.

When somebody calls me, I call them back, maybe not immediately, but I do call them back. I don't care how important my client is, or who the caller may be, they deserve a return call.

Also, if you're going to get something done, do it now. Do what you can immediately. That way, you can open yourself up to new opportunities and new circumstances.

While I am one of the easiest guys to get along with, I do hold other people responsible when they say they are going to do something. I don't get upset when they fail to follow through, but I do lecture them. I let them know that a phone call or text message would have been nice.

If you are not going to follow through on something, it is okay as long as you are proactive. Let others know if you can't meet a deadline, or if you aren't going to attempt a project in the first place. I'm not saying that you should make promises you aren't going to keep, but circumstances can come between you and your intent. When that happens, let people know. Be accountable for your words and actions.

With Maria Menounos of Extra *in the Brenden Celebrity Suite at Brenden Theatres at The Palms Casino Resort*

CHAPTER 39

A CAUTIONARY TALE

What's easy to get into is often hard to get out of, so proceed cautiously.

One day, a friend called me, and said, "Jerry, I need some advice. Do you have time? I want to run a couple things by you."

I said, "Absolutely."

He told me there was a gym near him that was for sale, and that the owner had debt. There was a movie theater connected to the gym, and because of this, my friend sought my advice.

My advice was to take the gym off the owner's hands, allowing him to walk away from it. In this case, my friend would assume the debt. Or, my friend could pay very little for the property and have the previous owner carry the debt. In this situation, my friend would pay on the debt over time.

"What do you think about the theater?" he asked. "Do you think you guys would be interested in it?"

I thought for a moment before offering, "We might be willing to do that if you changed the name of the theater to Brenden Theatres, and paid us $200,000 to manage it."

Well, that wasn't the music he wanted to hear. He was hoping we would partner with him in buying the business.

It turned out to be one of the worst investments of my friend's life. Four years later, he was trying to get out of it. Because the gym and theater took up so much of his time, he was unable to focus on other real estate investments that would take little of his time and yield good profits.

Eventually, he began to resent the investment because of the time and energy it took just to keep his head above water.

When a good opportunity comes around, investigate it. Do not make a decision based on emotion and ego. You have to step back and assess why they're selling, what you're buying, the debt involved, and who your audience is.

Even if a deal is too good to be true, how much effort will it take to give you the results you want? Moreover, could you be doing something better and more interesting with your time?

CHAPTER 40

STAN LEE'S GREATEST CREATION

I met Stan Lee at the *Iron Man* premiere at Brenden Theatre. It was a weekend event complete with the unveiling of his Brenden Celebrity Star, a banquet to raise money for his charity, and, of course, all the press that surrounds a premiere.

I didn't read comic books as a kid, so I wasn't aware of the impact Stan had already had on so many lives. I had certainly heard of many of his characters, such as Spider-Man, the Incredible Hulk, and, of course, Iron Man.

Friday evening before the Sunday premiere, Stan arrived in Las Vegas. I escorted him to the Playboy Club at the top of the Fantasy Tower of the Palms. I was amazed by the celebrity of this 80-year-old man who, besides creating superheroes and villains, had made many cameo appearances in his movies and a few television shows.

From that Friday night onward, Stan Lee realized I was in charge. Even with all his people around him, he still said, "I'll follow Jerry."

We unveiled Stan's Brenden Celebrity Star on Saturday, and then had a banquet and fundraiser for him in one

With Robert Downy Jr. at the Ironman *premier*

Stan Lee's Greatest Creation

of the ballrooms at the Palms Casino Resort. Again, it was revealing to see how excited the guests were to have the opportunity to honor Stan.

After the usual speeches and other ceremonies, I stepped up to the podium to announce the debut of a song that Stan Lee co-wrote, *That's L.A.* It was the first time the song had been performed before a crowd of that size. Stan was more than surprised that I not only had the idea to present the song, but that I had also gotten the band to perform it.

The next day, at the premiere, we surprised the audience with the appearance of Stan Lee. While most celebrities reluctantly promote their movies, Stan genuinely

With Stan Lee at the dinner celebrating his Brenden Celebrity Star

With Stan Lee's daughter, J.C. Lee, in her studio in Los Angeles

wants to interact with his fans. He is a gracious, humble man who has more energy than men half his age.

Over the past few years, I have built a strong personal relationship with Stan, his wife, and his daughter. In fact, you could say that I'm a close friend of the family. One day, I was contacted by Stan Lee's office. "Jerry, Stan would like to have you meet his daughter and represent her in some of her business ventures."

I recall seeing her at the event in Las Vegas two and a half years prior. I remember how she exuded style, fashion, and sophistication, and had a demeanor of being somewhat aloof. For that mere moment that I saw her, not only did she make a lasting impression, but I remember thinking, "WOW!" With the overwhelming attention that her father was receiving over the three days of events, I couldn't help but think how selfless an only child could be, sitting there with such grace after having shared her father with the world for her entire life. She truly is Stan's greatest creation.

Just over a year ago I was asked by the chairman of the board to join the Board of Directors for the Stan Lee Foundation, which promotes literacy. Of course, I accepted. It's amazing how things happen.

"In the time I've known Jerry he reminds me more and more of a bulldog. Once he gets a project between his teeth he just doesn't let up-which is an admirable quality for a celebrity publicist. Given a task, he lets nothing stand in the way of his accomplishing it. Hey, he even got me to write this paragraph! Good work, Jerry. Keep it up."

CNN Bureau, Los Angeles

CHAPTER 41

MICHAEL JACKSON COMMEMORATIVE BELT

When we were preparing for the Brenden Celebrity Star unveiling for Michael Jackson, I reached out to Simon, the owner of b.b. Simon Belts Worldwide. Johnny had an autographed *Thriller* album that he wanted to present in a private ceremony following the Brenden Celebrity Star unveiling. Johnny wanted to frame the album, and he envisioned something created by Simon.

I called Simon and described what Johnny wanted, and then I flew out to Newport Beach, California a couple days later to meet with him and discuss the details.

When I arrived at b.b. Simon's studio, I saw the most amazing works of art, the likes of which I had never seen before. For instance, there was a breathtaking grand piano encrusted with Swarovski elements that would have made Liberace jealous.

After touring me through his studio, Simon took me to lunch to discuss Johnny's frame.

It wasn't until we were heading back to his studio that Simon said to me, "Michael was a customer of mine. He bought a lot of things from my shop." Simon told me how one time, Michael wanted Simon to design a bedroom set, all with Swarovsky crystals—the headboard, footboard, the dresser, and everything else.

Simon said, "Unfortunately, he passed away. My family and I are big Michael Jackson fans, and I want to do something very special in his memory. I want to create a Michael Jackson Commemorative Belt."

Michael Jackson Commemorative Belt by b.b. Simon

He paused, "Jerry, I don't know the family. I don't have a relationship with them, but I know you do. I would like for you to become a partner with me on this venture. I will give you a portion of everything."

How could I say no?

When I got back to Vegas, I met with Johnny to tell him about his project with Simon. I also told him that Simon had asked me to help with his commemorative belt. I asked if it was okay with Johnny that I pursued the project.

Johnny said, "Yes. No worries."

That began a journey that we thought was going to take maybe a month or two, but has actually taken years.

As we began working on the Michael Jackson Commemorative Belt, we met with Katherine Jackson, and showed her different designs to get her input. Simon was ready with the first belt in a matter of weeks.

When we showed her the finished belt, she loved it. I said, "Mrs. Jackson, this is not about money."

She looked at the belt, smiled, and said, "I know this isn't about the money, Jerry. If it was, this should be selling for $5,000."

I then asked, "Mrs. Jackson, did you talk to the estate and get permission from them for us to sell the belts?"

"Yes I did."

I repeated, "So they are okay with this?"

She said, "Yes, they are."

Since she was a part of the estate as a beneficiary, we thought, "This is Michael's mother; you can't get any better assurance than that."

When the belt was completed, Simon and I met with Katherine in her Havenhurst home in Los Angeles. We presented belts to each of Michael's children, Prince, Paris, and Blanket. Mrs. Jackson signed a couple of them. The children signed a belt as well, which was the first and only item in the world that all three children had signed.

I specifically asked her again, "Mrs. Jackson, did you get approval from the estate?"

"Yes, I did."

I said, "Thank you."

I made sure that we launched the belt in a very big way, on *CNN Live*. Simon and I both appeared live with Alan Duke, the *CNN* entertainment reporter, and showed the belt to the world. Only 7,000 of these belts would ever be made. Once they were all sold, that would be it.

About an hour after we were off the set, Simon received an email from the estate commanding him to cease and desist. When Simon told me about the email, I said, "Okay, shut it down. There's some miscommunication here."

I wanted to make sure that we separated ourselves from the street vendors. This was the first and only item that Katherine Jackson had ever gotten behind in memory of her son. I wanted to make sure the world understood this, so I shut everything down immediately.

Moments later, I received a call from *TMZ*. "Jerry, I have some questions for you about this belt."

I said, "I'm sorry. I can't talk to you now. Feel free to email me."

Twenty minutes later, I received another phone call. "Jerry, I need seven seconds of your time."

I said, "Harvey, I apologize. I can't talk to you right now. I'm in the middle of another call. Please email me."

The reason I didn't take those calls is because, in a situation like that, it is important that you try to control it. If you are caught off-guard like I was, you don't want to talk to media until you have the facts straight.

The truth is I wanted to pack my bags and go home. But instead I stood tall and dealt with everything.

I had my associate, Joe Girouard, contact the attorney that sent the email. The attorney said, "Joe Jackson does not have the right to do this."

"No," I explained, "It's not Joe Jackson. It's Katherine Jackson."

That turned the tone of the conversation. "Oh, okay. Let me get back to you."

Me with La Toya Jackson, Simon, and Katherine Jackson

We never heard back. Months passed.

We had contacted Mrs. Jackson, and of course, she was surprised that we'd received the cease and desist letter.

I decided to sit back and let the dust settle.

In the interim, Mrs. Jackson had a couple different attorneys representing her. We met with those attorneys in regards to the belt. There were so many other things going on that the belt took a back seat. The problem was, Simon had already outlaid hundreds of thousands of dollars on this project on the assumption that we had the approval of the estate.

Months became years, and Mrs. Jackson obtained a new attorney, Perry Sanders. I tried to get a meeting with him for some time. Then, one afternoon, he called me and said, "Jerry, I'm going to be at Mr. Chow this evening. Why don't you come and meet with me? We'll have dinner at 8:00."

I said, "Yes. I will meet you there."

Well, I was home in Northern California when I got the call. I scrambled to pack and get to the Oakland International Airport. In three hours, I was in Beverly Hills, meeting with Perry.

I showed him the belt, and he said, "Jerry, you undersold it. This is unbelievable. It is the most beautiful thing I have ever seen. It is gorgeous. Yes, you should get a licensing agreement for it. It should be sold to the public."

Months went by before I got a phone call from Howard Weitzman, the attorney for the Michael Jackson Estate.

He knew about the belt, and suggested that we meet. Because of his vacation and an illness, it was several months before I went to his office in Santa Monica.

Was I intimidated to meet with Howard Weitzman? Yes. As far as I was concerned, this was one of the most important business meetings of my life. There were millions of dollars at stake, and I needed to make a good impression and gain Howard's confidence.

When I was ushered into his office, he was sitting behind a gigantic desk. After shaking hands and exchanging pleasantries, I showed him the belt. Then, I showed him a couple of catalogues of Simon's work, to make sure he understood the quality of the work.

Mr. Weitzman was impressed. He sat back, and we began to visit. I told him about my background, that I didn't live in Beverly Hills or Santa Monica, but that I was actually a former florist from Northern California.

When he heard about my former profession and where I live, he got a big grin on his face, "Jerry, I know who you are. I know what you did."

He then leaned forward, resting his elbows on the desk, "When that letter went out to cease and desist, we appreciate the way you shut everything down within moments. That spoke volumes about your character and who you are."

I said, "Thank you, Howard." (Earlier in the conversation he had asked me to do him a favor, and call him Howard.) "It was important to me that we separate ourselves from the street vendors. Had I known that I needed to go directly to you to get a licensing agreement, I promise you, I would have done it."

"I know that. I believe that, no doubt there," Howard said. "Let's see how we can move forward. Let's get this belt done. I am fully committed to it. It's not going to be a process since I am now personally involved. We're going to get it done for you."

As part of the settlement, Simon was allowed to sell the belts that he had completed, 7,000 in all. That equated to an $11.2 million deal that this second generation florist put together without hiring an attorney.

I just finished our meeting with Mr. Howard Weitzman, attorney for the Michael Jackson Estate. It was a proud day for me to meet with Howard, he is a good man, that was the beginning of establishing our relationship.

Better yet, I can now say that I have a good relationship with Howard Weitzman. He is a brilliant man. I don't believe that there is anyone else out there that could have done what he has done with the estate of Michael Jackson.

It was a long process, and there were plenty of naysayers along the way. Friends would say, "I keep hearing about this belt. You should put your efforts somewhere else, somewhere where you will get an immediate return on your investment."

Others suggested that I sue different people. But I knew that this would work out, and suing wasn't the answer. There was simply a miscommunication and the people at the Michael Jackson estate didn't understand, at first, what we had been doing, and how we had been working

Simon and Ne-oh at the presentation of the Michael Jackson Commemorative Belt to Ne-oh in New York City at NASDAQ

with Mrs. Jackson. Apparently, they were in the dark with this project. How could they have known?

I knew the project was significant, and I had the patience to see it through. I'd already visualized all 7,000 belts being sold. If you truly believe in something, if you feel the emotions of having what it is that you want, and if you are thankful for everything you have, the universe will manifest itself; it's simply the power of attraction.

Paris Jackson on stage in London honoring her father while wearing the bb simon Michael Jackson Commemorative Belt.

CHAPTER 42

BEING LET GO

One Friday night, I was out to dinner when I received a call from Johnny Brenden. "Jerry, do you have a minute? I'd like to talk to you."

"Can I call you back in a few moments?" I asked.

He said yes, and I went back to my car to call him.

Johnny started the conversation by saying, "This is hard. I'm going to have let you go."

Wow, that was a shock. It was the first time I had been without work since I was 13 years old.

"But I'll bring you back as an independent contractor. I'm going to increase your commission to 50%. I'm going to give you your car, plus I've put a package together for you. Of course, you will pay your own expenses."

As Johnny was talking, I was thinking, "What am I going to tell my family? My friends? How is this going to affect me? What will I do?"

At the time, I was the highest paid employee at Brenden Theatres. The CEO and CFO thought that by offering me an independent contractor deal, I would be motivated by greed to sell even more advertising.

The truth is, the move took all the wind out of my sails.

When I was working for Johnny Brenden, I did my job out of loyalty to him and the company, not for the money. Instead of motivating me by greed, they actually lost a key financial asset to their company.

Let my experience be a lesson. Never hang your hat on your job. You may think you are a financial asset to your company, but there are many reasons why they might let you go. Don't get all wrapped up in yourself and think that no one can replace you. After all, I was doing something no one had ever done with on-screen advertising, and it was only part of my job.

There are many reasons why you might lose your job.

The other lesson is to be nice to people on the way up, because you'll see them again on the way down.

As soon as word got out that I was a free agent, people want me to help them. Prior to being let go, I had refused everyone because I worked exclusively for Johnny.

I had built and maintained a great network. These relationships were so strong, they would be difficult to tarnish with a bulldozer. These were people who received cards from me on their birthdays. I knew what movies their children liked, and had sent them tickets for screenings. If they wanted or needed something, I did my best to provide it. Because of this attention, there were many important people in my network whom I could call on the phone, and they would take my call.

Within literally hours of being let go, I felt safe. I knew that my financial and professional futures were about to explode, not because of anything special about me, but because I had made sure that I was a potential asset to all the people I had met and worked with while at Brenden Theatres.

The good news is that I now have more time to spend with my family and friends. I breathe easier. I have a nice life. I could not enjoy these things without knowing the true value of my relationships.

In the end, I realized that, by nature, I am loyal. I would have never left Brenden Theatres, but I had outgrown the company. My position, as great as it was, was keeping me from all the opportunities available to me. In some small way, I think Johnny knew this as well.

Underlying my fear and determination, there was also a sense of relief when I was let go. A weight was taken off my shoulders. I viewed things differently from the moment I lost my job. I was in a business marriage headed for divorce, but I would have never been the one to leave.

When you're locked-in like that, you feel like you cannot leave. Worse, you feel trapped by your loyalty. You don't realize how miserable you are until you're given freedom.

It still hurts, and there is a lot of anxiety, but there is also a sense of relief.

When I got the severance papers, I couldn't sign them fast enough. By that time, I had a project in place with b.b. Simon Belts worth millions of dollars, and other lucrative projects were on the way.

I now work with some of the most amazing people on the planet, and enjoy every day of my life. I can choose to work on projects that engage my heart and soul.

When I go to a restaurant, people start talking to me. Because of my employment status, I can listen to their needs and suggest how I can help. The next thing you know, they give me large checks to work for them or give them advice. In the past, I would turn people away because of my exclusive relationship with Johnny and Brenden Theatres. Now that I don't work exclusively with one client, the world is my oyster.

At the end of the day, you are in charge of yourself. You can shape your destiny. You cannot leave it up to other people and hope they'll take care of you. Even though you are completely loyal to a company, it is business. If you rub someone the wrong way, or if they get jealous or offended, no matter how good you are at your job, it is always on the line. Don't think you are such an asset to the company that they'll never get rid of you. Jealousy, anger, and personalities cloud decision-making. After all, when someone else is in charge of your income, when you are working for others, the ball is in their court.

You can only be set for life if you set yourself up for life. You must take care of YOU first. Don't let your life be managed by somebody else. Be prepared at any time, so that if you lose a position, you can make a move in a different direction.

Months later, Johnny said to me, "I regret letting you go. I should never have let them talk me into it. That was the worst thing I've ever done." I do not harbor any resentment or hard feelings towards Johnny, and I will always have great respect and gratitude for him, and for Brenden Theatres. I continue to be an independent contractor for their company, and enthusiastically work with them throughout the year.

CHAPTER 43

GEORGE CLOONEY AND STAN LEE

Shortly after Johnny let me go, Stan Lee's people reached out to me. Stan was about to receive a star on the Hollywood Walk of Fame. Stan wanted my help because of the work I had done earlier with his Brenden Celebrity Star. After all, Stan told me, "Jerry, you're the best I've ever seen."

Of course, you want to do more than just hold a ceremony for the star, you also want to build it up with press appearances. So, I reached out to my friend Alan Duke, the Entertainment Reporter at *CNN*. I asked if he would interview Stan.

On the day of the interview, I left Stan in the green room while I attended to some details. When I returned, Stan was on the edge of the sofa, talking with George Clooney.

When I walked in, dressed as I normally am, George looked over and broke off the conversation in mid-sentence, "Uh oh. It just got serious," he said.

I smiled, "Nice to meet you again, Mr. Clooney."

"Call me George."

We began talking about the *Oceans 13* premiere that I had facilitated in Las Vegas. He remembered that Robin and Danny Greenspun donated one million dollars to Jerry Weintraub's charity that night.

At that moment, Alan Duke walked in to usher Stan Lee to the interview. Stan began walking with Alan, and then stopped and returned to the green room. He said, "Excuse me, you really are George Clooney?"

"Yes."

"I thought you were Alan Duke," Stan said.

The three of us laughed. Stan asked, "Can I get some pictures with you?"

"Sure," George smiled.

I took several pictures of the two of them together.

When Stan's interview was concluded, I asked that the president and chairman of the Stan Lee Foundation be interviewed to bring more attention to the foundation. Alan Duke agreed.

Hundreds of thousands of people learn to read through comics. It's an easy introduction to the world of reading for children. The Stan Lee Foundation wants to continue that tradition, and I wanted to make sure they had the opportunity to share their mission and vision with *CNN* viewers.

George Clooney in the CNN Los Angeles studios

After the interview, I was talking with Alan Duke, and he said, "Jerry, when Stan and I were walking out, he turned to me and asked, 'So you're Alan Duke? I thought I was just talking with Alan Duke.' Can you believe I was mistaken for George Clooney?"

To this day, Alan Duke still brags that George Clooney was mistaken for him.

With Alan Duke CNN outside court house at Conrad Murray trial

CHAPTER 44

SENDHERFLOWERS .COM

Donald Hotton created SendHerFlowers.com. When Donald first introduced the company to me, it made a lot of sense. The concept was to make it easy for men to buy flowers for women. The homepage asked a few questions, and within literally two minutes, flowers were on the way to the lady.

When Donald started the website, I wasn't involved, even though I thought I should be, especially after my experience with Global Florist. But Donald already had partners, so there wasn't a place for me on his team.

The project struggled to start for a couple years before it ended up sitting on the shelf.

Understanding the potential of his project, Donald pitched his website to a venture capitalist. The VC agreed to fund the project if he got a major percentage of the company.

Donald separated from his previous partners and turned over the marketing of SendHerFlowers.com to this venture capitalist.

After two more years with the venture capitalist, I called Donald to ask about how the project was going.
He said, "Well, my partner just launched it on Google."
"That's exciting. How many orders have you gotten?"
"Well, we haven't gotten any yet."
I said, "That's even more exciting."
"What do you mean?" Donald asked incredulously.
"Donald, you've been working on this for four years, and it hasn't come to fruition. The exciting thing about being launched with no orders is you can restart at ground zero. You've put in time, money, and effort. Your partner has working capital to invest. I will invest my expertise and resources. Because I know this industry very well, I will take you to the next level. But I want 55% percent of the company."
He said, "I'll talk to my partner. Let's do it."

We began working on the deal with emails and texts going back and forth. We spoke on the phone a few times, but months went by. Finally, I put Donald and his partner on the phone, to rejuvenate the project.
I asked for $10,000 in working capital up front because I wanted to cover and my expenses and I didn't want a dime coming out of my pocket. I bring a lot of value to the table, and $10,000 is minimal in the scheme of things; I just wanted a commitment from them to the value that I bring to the table.

It is important that you know that when you are creating a company, it is easy to put in money. The hard part is figuring out what you are going to do with it.

When you can bring a lifetime of cultivated relationships, and you can leverage them to help the business grow, that's priceless.

When it comes to business partnerships, I want to make sure that my partners are serious, and that they know the value of what I'm bringing to the table.

Don't let anyone tell you that if you're not bringing money, you don't get any shares. In fact, you should get a bigger share because people can't buy relationships. By bringing you onto their team, they now have access

I made Mrs. Katherine Jackson smile as this picture was taken. We were in her living room of her Calabasas Mansion. She was promoting new flower arrangements for SendHerFlowers.com

to the relationships you have cultivated. Normally, my consultation fee ranges from $5,000 up to $100,000, usually averaging $25,000 to $30,000.

People have come to me with their dream business model or desire. They only know what they know about their business and market, but they need help with marketing and public relations, or taking their idea to the next level.

I will have a conversation with them, and tell them that we need to know more about their business model. They will generally fly me to their city for a meeting. On that trip, they provide me with as much information as I need to make a decision.

If I like what I hear, and my research supports them, I will tell them I will help, but there are no guarantees.

I have a consultation fee, and it is non-refundable. They understand that I have spent years cultivating relationships, and that I can open doors for them, but it is up to them to keep their foot in the door.

Of course, people don't always have tremendous amounts of money, but they have a passion. They know it will take years to cultivate the relationships that they need, and they don't have that kind of time. When they engage with me, they can get to their goals a lot sooner.

When I was working with SendHerFlowers.com, the possibility of an app came up. I don't know much about this industry, so I brought in someone who would know if their idea made sense.

My person explained how an additional app would be helpful to the company, and I became interested.

But things kept moving slowly. I realized that by the time they launch the app, any technology they had would be out of date. So, I decided to get out. At that point, we had only lost our time.

When you're depending on someone else to row the boat, and they are very slow, you may want to get out. At the end of the day, if they're not able to show you how stable they are, then all your time and money is wasted.

Get in quick, see if it's viable. If it isn't, get out quick, and cut your losses.

CHAPTER 45

Hollywood Walk of Fame

Most people don't know that the stars on Hollywood Boulevard are sponsored. It costs $25,000 to get a star on the Walk of Fame. This is why some people you would think wouldn't be there are, and why others whom you'd think would be there aren't.

Once you've been approved for a star, you have four years to get it in the ground.

Stan Lee was approved for a star, but his people had fallen short. That is why they turned to me. My associate made some calls, and was able to resurrect Stan's application; otherwise, they would have had to start all over again.

When there is an unveiling, part of Hollywood Boulevard is shut down. A podium is set up, and the press assembles for the event. For all the preparation, the event itself is short.

The real celebration begins at the after-party. In Stan Lee's case, the reception was catered by Wolfgang's Steakhouse in Beverly Hills.

Stan Lee, of course, has a sizable Rolodex. While a lot of celebrities wanted to attend the party, we only had room

for 200. The goal for the event was to bring awareness to the Stan Lee Foundation.

The costs of an event like this are covered through sponsorships.

When I'm looking for sponsors for an event, I approach companies and propose that they either give money to be a sponsor, or provide a product or service for the event.

Companies want to be associated with things like the unveiling of Stan Lee's star. It's not necessarily about the 200 or so in attendance, but the shots that the paparazzi will publish. Their product will be featured at the event, and there will be pictures of celebrities enjoying their product. People will see that a product was at a prestigious event, and be inclined to buy the product themselves.

Unfortunately, someone had forgotten to arrange to have alcohol for the celebration.

I found out about this problem mere days before the event. It was rather late in the game to pick up liquor sponsors, but I started making calls.

First, I called Southern Wine and Spirits, a major distributor. No one at the company could find someone who could make a decision, so they told me they'd contact me on Monday, the day before the reception.

There wasn't much I could do over the weekend, but as soon as Monday came around, I was back on the phone with Southern Wine and Spirits. They offered some alcohol, but not enough for the whole event.

That wasn't acceptable.

Stan Lee had made a cameo appearance on the show *Entourage* a few months prior, and Avion tequila had been featured in the storyline the prior season. I knew how important the relationship between Stan Lee, POW! Entertainment, and Avion is. So, I reached out to them for the unveiling.

They agreed to provide the tequila. Within 24 hours they delivered several cases, and they threw in a beautiful ice sculpture as well.

Lou Ferrigno with me at the after party.

I needed more than just tequila, so I reached out to a friend of mine who owns a vodka company, Johnny Matheany. I said, "Johnny, I need your help. Can you provide some cases of vodka for the Stan Lee Foundation reception?"

"Jerry, I have this great vodka, Devotion."

Buzz Aldrin and me at the after party for the Stan Lee Star on the Hollywood walk of fame at Wolfgang's steakhouse in Beverly Hills.

I had to ask, "Is that the vodka from "The Situation" of *Jersey Shore*?"

"Well, I own it. He represents it."

"Here's the catch," I said. I want your vodka, but we cannot have any signage associated with your product because of an agreement with Avion Tequila.

Me and Jerry West of the NBA

He said, "Don't worry about it, Jerry. I will bring you the cases."

For all of the last minute wrangling, it was a flawless event. No one knew about the last-minute dealings, nor how close we came to not having alcohol at the event. I could not have pulled this off without strong relationships and associations.

Ronny Turiaf, me, Adonal Foyle, and Neda Barrie

Chapter 46

Going Back to Indiana, Can You Feel It?
Michael Jackson's Celebration

One January morning, I received a phone call from Lowell Henry, the business advisor to Katherine Jackson. "Jerry, this is what you've got."

"Yes."

"Katherine just got off the phone with the mayor of Gary, Indiana, and she told the mayor that she wants you to represent her this year for the Michael Jackson Birthday celebration in Gary."

"That would be an honor," I said.

"You'll need a budget. What do you think? I'm thinking $200,000."

"I can work with that." He continued, "We want you to put four days of events together. You are the official person, and everybody will take your lead."

Of course, I was humbled. What a great honor to be asked. Mrs. Jackson could have asked anybody to do this, but she reached out to me.

Lowell continued, "Call the mayor. Get an appointment. Go down there, meet with her, and put it together. When you have everything lined up the way you want it, come out to Calabasas and have a meeting with Mrs. Jackson to go over everything.

"And, most important," he continued, "You have to put together an itinerary for the kids. Last year, they had nothing to do."

This was the third birthday celebration after Michael's death. The program developers in the past were so involved with getting money for the event that they forgot about the kids.

All I could say was, "Great."

I called the mayor's office and made an appointment for a conference call with her team and my associate, Joe Girouard. From there, the event began to come together.

Days later, I sat down with Mrs. Jackson and told her, "I've come up with the title for the event: Going Back to Indiana: Can You Feel It?"

Going Back to Indiana was a song recorded live by the Jackson 5 at Roosevelt High School in Gary, Indiana. *Can You Feel It* is the title of a popular Michael Jackson song.

Mrs. Jackson loved my idea.

The plans progressed to the point that I needed to visit Gary to meet with the mayor. While I was there, Reverend Jesse Jackson was speaking at a Chamber of Commerce function I had been invited to.

I made sure I to take the opportunity to meet with him before taking a tour of the city.

In the backyard of Michael Jackson's childhood home looking at his koi fish. Lowell Henry, Mr. Joe Jackson right before the Oprah interview.

Later in the day, we had a meeting with the city officials, including over twenty people from different concerned groups, like the police and fire departments.

I sat at the head of a huge boardroom table, and everyone was looking at me, waiting for me to talk. They looked like they were loaded for bear. People in the past had promised them many things, and none of them had panned out. I could feel their defensiveness. They felt duped by all the unfulfilled promises of the past.

I realized they were waiting for me to speak. I took a breath and said, "It is my privilege and pleasure to be here. I officially represent Katherine Jackson, the mother of Michael Jackson, the greatest entertainer that ever lived. I want to create a four-day celebration worthy of his contribution. And I'm going to promise you nothing."

Then, I laid out my plan. "We'll start with a candle-light vigil honoring Michael's passing. Then, there will be a dinner hosted by Mrs. Jackson at the Majestic Star Casino. This will be followed by a performance at Roosevelt High School for the community."

I paused and looked everyone in the eye. "The buck stops with me. I'm going to under-promise and over-deliver. My goal is to leave people wanting more, so that we can lay the foundation for a bigger event next year."

I think I deflated the people who were there to complain. In previous years, people had come to Gary and misrepresented themselves and the city. Things didn't work out very well. Now, there was hope that this year would be different.

When I returned to California, Lowell contacted me to let me know that the budget was now $150,000. Later still, it was lowered to $100,000. Then $50,000.

Finally, he called me and said, "Jerry, I can't get you any dough. This event will have to be self-funded. You have to get sponsors."

"That's fine," I said.

As soon as I began looking for sponsors, I got a call to see if we could get Prince Jackson to make an all expenses paid appearance. The interested party only wanted him to make a ten-minute presentation about the legacy of his father. In return, the company would not only pay all expenses, including chartering a private jet for Prince, his personal security, and his guardians, but they would also contribute $15,000 towards the Michael Jackson celebration in Gary, Indiana.

I presented the opportunity to Lowell, and he said he'd get back to me. Months went by with me occasionally calling to get an update, but I didn't hear from him.

So, we lost that opportunity.

Next, I met with a producer who wanted to do a documentary about the Jackson kids that would be sold to a prime-time network. He wanted to show how the Jackson family was giving back to the community of Gary, Indiana.

They put together a contract in which the producer would put up $25,000 in good faith plus $50,000 at the signing of the contract. It would be enough to make the event happen.

After meeting with the producer, I contacted Lowell Henry for his guidance, and to ask him to present the opportunity to Mrs. Jackson. Mrs. Jackson signed the contract allowing them to film. This was days before all of us went out to Gary for the event.

After I had met with Katherine Jackson at her Calabasos home, and laid out the detailed, itemized itinerary for the four days of events, and a detailed itinerary of the festivities for Michael's children over those four days, she agreed to the plan. Lowell then asked, "Jerry, can the flight for you and Joe be paid for out of the sponsorships instead of having Katherine pay for them?"

I agreed, knowing that I had been promised a check that would cover the expenses for the four days of events.

The plan was that the kids would ride to Gary on a tour bus, but when the camera crew arrived at the bus, they found out that the kids would be flying. The crew quickly arranged to be on the same plane as the kids, so they could film them arriving in Gary.

When they arrived, however, the kids were ushered off the plane out of sight of the cameras.

I had arranged for the kids to go to an amusement park for the day, but it looked like it was going to rain. So, instead, Lowell arranged for them to tour Harpo Studios, Oprah's operation. The kids enjoyed it, but, in the meantime, it turned out to be one of the nicest days ever.

The kids decided they wanted to go to the amusement park after all. The problem was, we were with security and no one had any money. They kept asking me to cover everything. Since I believed I would be getting a check soon from the producers, I gladly paid.

Days prior, I had received a phone call from Jeffrey, La Toya Jackson's business partner, asking if La Toya could join us in Gary for the celebration. Of course, I said yes.

I then found out that she had just begun filming her reality show with the *OWN Network*, and that she would be bringing her camera crew to film during the four days of events.

The celebration went off flawlessly. The tribute began with a candlelight vigil on Wednesday, the 29th of August, which was Michael's birthday. We gathered in front of the Jackson house on 2300 Jackson Street.

I had invited Reverend Jesse Jackson to open the ceremony that evening, and he graciously accepted. It was an honor for e to introduce him to the audience, along with La Toya Jackson.

The following day, Thursday, Prince and Paris threw out the first ball at the RailCats baseball game. The RailCats are Gary's farm team.

Friday, we had a sit-down dinner for 250 people at the Majestic Star Casino. Mrs. Jackson attended the event, and we had some wonderful performers entertaining the guests.

Finally, on Saturday, we held a concert in a theater connected to a high school that seated 2,000 people. Since so many of the events cost money, we gave away most of the tickets to the community, so that they could participate in the tribute. This was important to Mrs. Jackson. She didn't want the four days to be just for the media dignitaries. She gave blocks of tickets to the Boys and Girls Club to distribute. That way, people who wouldn't normally be able to afford to bring out their entire family for the evening could attend.

I'm giving a thumbnail sketch of all that went on, but it's important to say that the four days went almost flawlessly thanks to the amount of attention to detail that we put in. Keep in mind, we had been working on this project for nearly six months. My associate, Joe Girouard, stayed up nightly until 3:00 or 4:00 in the morning updating the schedule of events. All he had to work with was a 12-year-old computer in the hotel where we were staying.

With Reverend Jesse Jackson in Gary, Indiana

Let me clarify that it takes a team, it takes an army, to put together an event like this. Yes, I was representing Katherine Jackson, but I had a team to help execute my vision.

I have an associate, Joe Girouard, who is a tremendous asset to me. He does what I don't like to do. I do what he doesn't like to do. We are a good team.

In addition, our efforts were also supported by the staff of the Mayor and people like Chuck Hughes, the executive director of the Chamber of Commerce in Gary. There were also a number of people that I don't have the space to acknowledge here who were extremely vital in making the events possible.

For all the work and stress we put into the events, we were exhilarated because we knew we were a part of history.

I was also humbled. How did this florist become the person representing Michael Jackson's mother, and coordinating one of the best tributes to his life? And not only did I work with the Mayor and other town officials of Gary, and Katherine Jackson and her staff, but I also worked with Michael's children and their security. When I think of all that I accomplished and experienced, I can't fathom where I've come in my life. It just goes to show that you can do anything you want to do.

When I got back to Northern California, I drafted thank-you letters to all those who helped make the event a success.

At the end of the day, it is very important that you work well with your team. Everyone must have the same agenda and have the same desire to put on a successful event. It is your job, as the leader, to tap into people's strengths.

Remember, there is no "I" in team. If everyone executes a great project, then everyone should take credit for its success. It is important that you recognize all those who contribute to your projects.

CHAPTER 47

FIRST ANNUAL GIANTS' *STAN LEE DAY* AT AT&T PARK

I was in San Francisco meeting with a colleague. We were discussing putting together an awards show for Stan Lee. Near the end of our meeting, my colleague, Mike, said, "Jerry, I have a good friend who works for the San Francisco Giants. He has tried to do a Stan Lee Day at their ballpark for years, but to no avail."

I said, "Have your friend call me and I'll make it happen for him."

That evening I got a call from Mike's friend, Faham of the San Francisco Giants. We set up an appointment for the following day.

Joe Girouard flew out for the meeting, and we met with Faham and several other people in the San Francisco Giants' boardroom.

I opened the discussion by letting everyone know that I have a personal relationship with Stan Lee, and that he is also a producing partner with me in a TV show we are creating.

They shared with me their desire to have a Stan Lee Day at AT&T Park, and, more importantly, that they would like it to be an annual event.

I told them I would talk with Stan and see what we could put together. I asked them to give us a few dates to choose from. Of course, there would be some costs associated with the event. I asked what their financial contribution would be. They told me their budget, and I agreed to see what I could do.

After the meeting, I called Stan Lee. I told him what the San Francisco Giants wanted to do, and how much they could pay him for the appearance.

He said, "That's fine, Jerry. Just let me know what the details are."

Shortly after we hung up, Stan called back. "Jerry, you did say you'd pay me..." and he repeated my figure back to me.

"Yes."

"My fees are much higher than that."

"Okay, Stan. What would you like?"

Stan told me what he would normally charge for such an appearance. "I would do it for you for less, but that is the fee I would prefer."

"Don't worry about it, Stan. I will make sure you get your fee."

To put this in perspective, Stan Lee travels the world to do signings. He commands between $60 to over $200 per person to appear at these events, not because he's greedy,

Stan Lee at AT&T Park

Stan Lee with Sergio Romo

Stan Lee Day

but because he is that great of a man, and people appreciate him that much. The San Francisco Giants didn't have that kind of a budget, but Stan still wanted to support them.

I immediately called my associate Joe and laid out the situation. "What do you think?"

"Jerry, not a problem. We can get him that money. We will need sponsors. Let's lay the groundwork next week."

We then discussed what we would need to do to garner the funds thStan was requesting. We contacted a popular comic book store in the Bay Area to set up a signing for that particular day, prior to the game. We immediately hired an artist to create a poster for the event that would feature Stan Lee and Sergio Romo as a super hero. Stan and Sergio would sign a limited number of these posters to raise the value of the experience for those paying to see Stan Lee at the ballpark.

After the conversation with Joe, I called Stan back. "We have everything in place. Let me know the day that would work best for you, and we'll get this scheduled."

It's also important to let you know that Stan has a guy who works for him on many of his events. This guy makes a lot of money taking Stan around and setting things up for him. Stan trusts him, and, on a personal note, I appreciate someone who looks out for Stan.

In a later meeting with Stan, he said, "Jerry, you know I usually work with..." and mentioned the man, "But I also work with other people where he is not involved."

I said, "I understand that, and I do not want to get in the way of anything. However, I would like to bring you other opportunities that he may not be able to. As you know, people often come to me with offers that I would like to bring to you. I will only mention them if you're okay with it."

Stan smiled, as only Stan can, and said, "Please, bring me anything. This project does not require anyone else but you."

There had been some confusion with people wanting to circumvent me on this event, but in the end, Stan is always a gentleman. He called me and said, "Jerry, I am going to do this, only for you."

This was a relationship event. Stan knows that I live in Northern California, so he did this as a personal favor.

The event was a huge success. The Giants said it was one of the most enjoyable and successful events they ever held. In fact, I am in conversation right now with the Giants organization to create a huge Stan Lee Day for next year.

The point is if you are steadfast and deliberate in your convictions, you will prevail. Don't let anyone stand in your way, and remember that it's better to include rather than exclude. When you get more people on your team, you have a better chance of executing your vision successfully.

The lesson for you is to never let anyone bully or intimidate you. If they fail to have an understanding of a situation, but if you have successfully conveyed your understanding, then it becomes their problem. Move on, and stay focused.

CHAPTER 48

LOOKING BACK, LOOKING FORWARD

As I read back over what I've written here, I want to make sure that you understand that it hasn't all been good in my life. Mistakes have been made and tragedies have occurred, but I don't focus on them.

When I was young, working at Jory's Flowers in Walnut Creek, there was this gentleman who would come by the shop and buy several hundreds of dollars in flowers at a time. In the early 1980s, that was a lot of money. It's still a lot of money for flowers.

I can remember his beautiful Rolls Royce pulling up outside the shop.

He was a very dynamic gentleman, and adventurous. He'd tell us about wild boar hunting, falconing, and the different excursions he'd been on.

One day, Duane Hotton, said to him, "Hey, you tell us about your success; tell about some of your failures."

The man didn't miss a beat. He proclaimed, "You will hear of my successes, but you will not hear of my failures."

I think he meant that he does not dwell on failures. I make that my goal. My focus is on the ball, and I will continue to move forward. Have I had some failures? Absolutely. Have I made some mistakes? Many. Do I dwell on them? Absolutely not.

If I make a mistake, I learn from it. I do my best to never make that mistake again. Have I made the same mistake a couple of times? Absolutely. But I brush myself off and continue to move forward. I need to excel, and I need to execute my desires. At the same time, I will learn. As they say, when you know better, you do better. And when you learn, teach.

Everybody has opportunities to succeed in life. Everybody has opportunities to make mistakes. Don't let your mistakes overwhelm you. Don't let them cloud your desires. Continue to continue. Believe in yourself.

I think back to the third grade when my mom told me that I can do anything I want. But she did more than just tell me that, she guided me on how to obtain it, while being appreciative for everything. She taught me to imagine where I wanted to be, and then feel the emotion of having received what I wanted.

Back then, I followed in my father's footsteps. I knew I was going to become a florist and own my own flower shop, but I became more than just a florist. I ended up excelling in my field, and achieving more than any other florists in my market.

While working toward becoming a florist, I met the publicist to a millionaire, and I wanted to be that guy. I became him, and more.

All roads will lead to your destination. I attribute my path to my zodiac sign, Cancer. I am a crab, and crabs aren't going to get anywhere by going in a straight line. They go sideways, crooked, here and there. But they eventually get to where they want to go.

At the end of the day, I ultimately achieve my goals.

I didn't do it alone. Important people helped me along the way. For instance, Duane Hotton, the owner of Jory's Flowers, taught me about business. He was a smart businessman and he paid his employees very well. Because he took care of his employees, he had little turn-over.

Duane taught me how to purchase flowers, and how to negotiate for the best price. His motto was, "If you will take care of your business, your business will take care of you."

And where would I be without Greg Warner? He instilled in me the importance of putting together a strong and detailed pro forma, a business plan. If you have a plan, you can work toward your goal. Greg is a very conservative man, and that also helped balance things out for me.

Of course, Johnny Brenden instilled in me the importance of follow-through. He also told me that I could only be star-struck for one year. After that, I had to be humble, and stay humble. He knew the people that I would be meeting, the places I would be going, and the experiences I would be having, such as being chauffeured everywhere, driving in Lamborghinis, eating at the finest restaurants, staying at the finest five-star hotels, and shopping at places like Barney's, Saks Fifth Avenue, Versace, Louis Vuitton, Pucci, and Gucci. Through it all, he wanted to make sure I stayed humble. All that can go to one's head, but I knew my place and whom I worked for.

It has been an amazing life, and I have lots of living left to do. I'm excited to discover what the future will bring. As Johnny Brenden recently said, "Jerry, everybody likes a good comeback.

TO BE CONTINUED...

Please visit my website: www.JerryOlivarez.com

www.ingramcontent.com/pod-product-compliance
Lightning Source LLC
Chambersburg PA
CBHW071704160426
43195CB00012B/1572